Global Flashpoints 2017

Global Flashpoints 2017

Editors

Craig Cohen

Josiane Gabel

CSIS | CENTER FOR STRATEGIC & INTERNATIONAL STUDIES

ROWMAN & LITTLEFIELD
Lanham • Boulder • New York • London

Center for Strategic & International Studies
1616 Rhode Island Avenue, NW
Washington, DC 20036
202-887-0200 | www.csis.org

Published by Rowman & Littlefield
A wholly owned subsidiary of The Rowman & Littlefield Publishing
Group, Inc.
4501 Forbes Boulevard, Suite 200, Lanham, MD 20706
www.rowman.com

Unit A, Whitacre Mews, 26-34 Stannary Street, London SE11 4AB

ISBN: 978-1-4422-7986-5 (cloth alk. paper)
ISBN: 978-1-4422-7987-2 (paperback)
ISBN: 978-1-4422-7988-9 (electronic)

Contents

1. WHAT ARE THE MAIN NATIONAL SECURITY CHALLENGES FACING THE TRUMP ADMINISTRATION?

John J. Hamre

The greatness of a democratic political system is that there is legitimacy with change. When an authoritarian government changes leaders, there is always uncertainty of what it means and what will happen. This year, in the United States, Donald Trump won a legitimate election and is now president-elect.

This was an election that showed how unhappy Americans are with how Washington has performed over the past two administrations. Both political parties adopted postures of obstruction and inaction. The Bush administration decried Democratic congressional obstructionism, and the Obama administration rails at Republican intransigence. The American people became increasingly angry with both parties. President-elect Trump captured those popular sentiments, and in many ways his election represents a hostile takeover of the Republican Party.

President-elect Trump's campaign was more about projecting sentiment than championing specific policy formulas. Building a wall on the southern border and making Mexico pay for it was a sentiment, not a plan. His supporters knew that, while traditional internationalists hung on the specific words as though they constituted real policy direction. Voters wanted to sweep away the stale politics of Washington, but the country still needs the structure and discipline of solid government operations.

Now the sentiment of the Trump campaign has to be translated into concrete policies by the incoming Trump administration. That takes a knowledge of government and how it functions. It takes a knowledge of the historic context for pending issues, and an understanding of the forces that must be accommodated in new policy formulations. The global nature of business and communications today means that America has to be knowledgeable about the outside world and understand that the actions occurring in other countries have a direct impact on our lives and well-being. The new administration will need substantive ideas and quality analysis more than ever.

So what are the principal national security challenges facing the Trump administration when it takes over in January 2017? Below I outline four. These are not the types of problems that will show up in the President's Daily Brief his first day in office, such as defeating ISIS, addressing insecurity in Syria, or dealing with a nuclear-armed North Korea. These are issues that will create the underlying dynamics that will yield either crisis or opportunity in the years ahead, shaping not only the success of a Trump administration, but also the vitality of America through numerous administrations to come.

FIRST, OUR DOMESTIC SITUATION

Our politics has deteriorated, the government is bloated, our economy is stagnant, and our country is divided. These will all have significant impact on our nation's security.

Other countries look to America's ability to do big things, to follow words with deeds, to act with efficiency and purpose, and to effectively resource our strategies. When we fail to do these things, either because of a lack of capacity or will, other countries perceive it as a sign of weakness. Allies hedge and adversaries are emboldened.

I have often felt that America's power primarily reflected the vitality of its domestic society and economy. Think of what our country could do—and the signal it would send abroad—if a Trump administration could build domestic political consensus on creating jobs, reforming taxes, strengthening education and skills training, rebuilding infrastructure, streamlining regulations, and making government more efficient. While these are all domestic issues, leaders and populations around the world watch us intensely. If our country can solve real problems domestically over the next four years, our international standing and influence will rise dramatically.

To take one example, the Trump campaign has indicated a desire to free the Defense Department from sequestration, the automatic spending cuts imposed after the debt-ceiling crisis of 2011. Sequestration has been harmful and should be ended, but its removal will depend on the Trump administration's ability to find a broadly based consensus on how revenues and resources will be balanced in the years ahead. To date, the parties have promoted only their solution to the structural financial problems the government faces. Durable policy outcomes depend on compromise.

What makes this type of compromise so difficult today is that Congress has dramatically weakened itself by taking the substance out of governing. True power in Washington comes when we harness politics to governing. You govern effectively to win the next election. Today it is politics without governing. Votes are symbolic statements designed to shape the next election. If this continues, we will become little more than a paper tiger in the eyes of the world.

SECOND, AMBIVALENT ALLIES

Much has been made of the Trump campaign's tough talk about allies. Candidate Trump essentially characterized allies in Europe, Asia, and the Gulf as "free riders" (echoing the same sentiments articulated by President Obama in an interview this summer). The implication was that America alone is carrying the burdens of maintaining an international order, and that we ought to stop that and start to put the burden on other countries that have benefited from our leadership but not paid their fair share for the security we provide.

It is unclear how President Trump will deal with allies or how he values them. Perhaps he does value allies but simply seeks leverage to exert a greater commitment on their part, something many former U.S. officials have called for publicly and privately. We simply don't know.

The central strategy developed for winning the Cold War—building alliances to share the burden of defense and to establish a normative world order—remains valid and useful. We are committed to defending others so that we will not have to defend ourselves in isolation. The security challenges we face today may be less existential than during the Cold War, but they are dramatically more complex. I cannot think of a single threat we face as a nation that is easier to handle with no allies.

But what happens if our allies and partners assess the value they perceive in their relationship with the United States and find us lacking? Life is filled with examples of key partnerships that are not perfectly reciprocal, and of divergent perspectives concerning who benefits more from a given relationship. What happens if countries begin to doubt our nuclear umbrella, or if the absence of an economic strategy in Asia pushes countries closer to Beijing, or if Europe begins to disintegrate as a cohesive whole, or if Gulf partners look for an alternative guarantor of regional security? None of these scenarios would be good for the United States.

Although candidate Trump believed getting tough with allies would come across as a sign of strength during the campaign, President Trump may conclude that such rhetoric contributes to allied skepticism about American commitment to shared security burdens, further eroding the foundation of America's strategy to lead a network of countries with shared perceptions of mutual interest. How do we reinvigorate that network to more effectively deal with today's security challenges?

THIRD, MORE ASSERTIVE REGIONAL COMPETITORS

What makes the prospect of ambivalent allies particularly worrisome is the way regional competitors such as China, Russia, and

Iran have become more assertive in recent years. These countries have developed methods for challenging U.S. primacy below a threshold that could trigger an overt U.S. response. This has been called ambiguous warfare, hybrid warfare, and "gray zone" activity.

This gray zone activity has integrated cyber espionage, covert operations, psychological operations, promotion of insurgency elements, subtle military maneuvers, and political and economic subversion into a seamless whole. The doctrine goes well beyond traditional defense activities. It starts with covert means of corrupting politicians in target countries. Because we don't readily see the visible manifestation of this malfeasance and because it purposefully stays below a certain threshold, we have not been quick to take action. Long-standing redlines are rendered meaningless. We know what to do if one of our allies is invaded, but it is more ambiguous if a mysterious commercial entity buys a dodgy bank and uses the bank to corrupt local politicians of an allied country. This is not warfare, but the net effect has been a loss of U.S. influence in Asia, Europe, and the Middle East.

We have the additional problem that our government is not well organized to recognize and address this problem. The threat crosses traditional boundaries between defense, diplomacy, and public diplomacy; between overt activity and espionage; and between security and economics. During the Cold War we were better at taking a comprehensive approach because there was consensus on the enemy at hand. No such consensus exists today. This is infinitely more complicated than the Cold War. It takes a far more sophisticated and integrated response than what we have mounted to date.

FOURTH, THE SECURITY IMPLICATIONS
OF THE COMMUNICATIONS REVOLUTION

The communications revolution—my shorthand for the technological developments that continue to reshape our lives—has had an enormous effect on traditional national security approaches, and will become even more important in the years ahead.

At the most basic level, there is the vulnerability of the country's secure information and infrastructure. Lost beneath the politicized rhetoric of this issue during the campaign is a very real danger that could present itself if adversaries were ever to gain access or exert control over, say, U.S. nuclear command and control, our banking system, or our electrical grid. History has proven that it is easier to play offense than defense in the cyber realm, which is cause for concern.

Beyond cybersecurity, we have also witnessed the role that modern communications play in the plotting, motivation, and radicalization of terrorists who seek to do us harm. The lack of trust between the U.S. government and U.S. private sector has made addressing this problem of surveilling and thwarting attacks particularly difficult. Each side sees "security" or "privacy" in maximalist terms, making sensible compromise impossible.

Finally, more indirect but no less significant, we see how modern communications tools have allowed individuals around the world to eschew established institutions, channels, and norms. This is at root democratic and liberating, but it also has had the undesired effect of eroding government's ability to respond adequately to events and craft timely, credible responses. Governments will never be nimble enough to keep up with the pace of modern communications. This naturally gives nongovernmental adversaries an edge when interests diverge.

LOOKING AHEAD

These four broad challenges will shape the nature of the crises and opportunities that arise over the next four years. In this publication, CSIS experts seek to flesh out specific policy areas that the new administration will likely face. I cannot recall another time when an incoming administration faced more questions at home and abroad. The complexity of the challenge is immense.

The job of the president has always been to help America survive as a nation and prosper as a people. But it has never been only about us. The United States has always been the world's hope for a better world. We are a nation that led the fight against fascism and communism, the fight against poverty and oppression. The responsibility is great and our record imperfect, but when it matters most, we have been up to the task. There is no reason to think we will not be in the years ahead.

When Senator Bob Dole received the Presidential Medal of Freedom from President Bill Clinton, only weeks after he lost to him at the polls, he made the following statement:

"Our challenge is not to question American ideals, or replace them, but to act worthy of them. . . . If we remember this, then America will always be the country of tomorrow, where every day is a new beginning and every life an instrument of God's justice."

To act worthy of America's ideals: this is the most serious challenge that any of us truly face.

2. IS THE FOUNDATION OF THE U.S.-LED ORDER CRUMBLING?

Michael J. Green

Director of National Intelligence James Clapper spoke for many policy and intelligence professionals when he recently described the current international security environment as "the most complex and diverse array of global threats" he has faced in his 53 years in the intelligence business. American victories seem rare, painfully won, and often fleeting. In contrast, Russia, China, Iran, and North Korea have been mounting multipronged assaults on cyberspace, outer space, and in the gray zones around Central Europe and the South China Sea with seeming impunity. Meanwhile, globalization has unleashed the specter of climate change and pandemics that would be beyond the ability of single governments to control. And just when the world's leading democracies should be rallying to these new challenges, they are hobbled at home by a new wave of nativism and populism as domestic institutions continue to disappoint populations struggling with growing inequality and the diminishing returns of the social welfare state.

Are the foundations of the current U.S.-led global order themselves at risk in this more challenging environment? Over the past 70 years, the United States has underwritten international stability and prosperity by leveraging the capacity and willpower of the American people; a global network of bilateral and multilateral alliances; the gradual expansion of human freedom; and a global institutional architecture that has encouraged trade, growth, and the incorporation of rising powers. As John Ikenberry of Princeton has noted, the United States is a "liberal leviathan" that has sustained leadership by sharing leadership—even as the American share of global GDP has slipped from 50 percent after the Second World War to 25 percent after the Vietnam War and 23 percent today.

The most important of these foundations remains the capacity and willpower of the American people to lead. It is for this reason that the free world watched the 2016 U.S. presidential election with such angst. Polling around the world suggests that America's closest allies, including Japan and Australia, increasingly see the United States in decline. Gains made in the "rebalance" to Asia are being offset by the recent hedging and defections by countries like the Philippines, Thailand, and Malaysia. Internal populism and nationalism are playing a role in these countries, but so too are the doubts being sown by America's slow response to coercion in the South China Sea, the sudden opposition to the Trans-Pacific Partnership (TPP) by both presidential candidates, and the outright attacks on allies by one candidate in particular. It remains to be seen whether these attacks by President-elect Trump are merely campaign rhetoric, an attempt to build leverage, or actually reflect disregard for the current alliance system.

Yet there are compelling reasons why American leadership is in fact much more resilient than the growing narratives at home and abroad suggest. The first is economic. In 2001 Goldman Sachs issued its first "BRICS" report arguing that Brazil, Russia, India, China, and South Africa would dominate global growth and investment in the coming decades. In the aftermath of the 2008 global financial crisis, that prediction seemed likely to accelerate, but in 2015 Goldman Sachs shut down its "BRICS" investment fund as the United States remained in the commanding position of top host for foreign direct investment globally thanks to unmatched innovation and energy self-sufficiency, while the BRICS countries struggled with corruption, lower energy prices, and stifling obstacles to innovation.

Of course, the confidence of international investors in the U.S. economy is not matched by the American public, which feels growing disparities in income distribution and thinks the country is going in the wrong direction by a two-to-one margin. Still, the internationalism of the American people has been far more resilient than the current political cycle suggests. Recent polls show that a majority of Americans still support free trade, and it is likely that the intensity of key interest groups with respect to trade has amplified the opposition to TPP in this presidential election year, without necessarily reflecting a broader or irreversible turn against international economic engagement in the country. President-elect Trump's criticism of U.S. allies, meanwhile, could be derivative of broader dissatisfaction with the political establishment, but it is hardly the expression of some popular new groundswell against standing side by side with historic democratic allies on the front lines. More Americans than ever believe that the United States should defend Japan or Korea if they are attacked in Asia. Only about half of Americans have positive views of the North Atlantic Treaty Organization (NATO), but that has been a fairly consistent number since the end of the Cold War.

Meanwhile, though American alliances have been badly shaken by more nativist and populist politics at home and some uncertainty about American willpower in the South China Sea, the Persian Gulf, and Central Europe, the trend lines are still largely positive. Public support for alliances is generally higher among America's leading treaty partners around the world (even the Philippines), and most of the major security relations are becoming more joint and interoperable. Japan has revised its interpretation of Article Nine of the Constitution to strengthen "seamless" operations with U.S. forces; Korea has put off reclaiming wartime operational control from the United States and is instead focusing on more effective joint planning for responses to escalations by the North. Though slow off the dime, NATO is now bolstering forces in the Baltics and Eastern Poland to counter a more assertive Russia. The United States is also enjoying deeper defense cooperation with India, and in East Asia the system of bilateral alliances established in the 1950s is increasingly networked as Japan, Korea, Australia, India, and others deepen their respective bilateral and trilateral security cooperation.

These increasingly networked, interoperable, and integrated alliances are a response to our allies' growing concerns regarding regional rivals like Russia or China that are using coercion to change the status quo. The question is whether the enhancement of security alliances and partnerships is sufficient. Jointness is arguably as important to deterrence as aggregate spending on military capability, but that said, only 5 of NATO's 28 countries have met the alliance's agreed 2 percent of GDP spending on defense. And while Japan has increased defense spending in recent years, it still spends less than 1 percent of GDP on defense. Since 2011, China and Russia have increased defense spending by about 30 percent, while the United States has cut defense spending by about a fifth. The United States and its allies still enjoy a significant qualitative edge over any potential regional adversary, but have lost leverage as these regional competitors have demonstrated greater aptitude at asymmetrical targeting of forward bases, space and cyber networks, and a higher tolerance for risk in gray zone tests of will than the United States or our allies have been able to muster. Then there is the additional challenge posed as North Korean nuclear developments threaten the credibility of American extended deterrence and readiness for risk in response to military provocations short of war.

Yet it is important to reiterate that none of these more emboldened regional players have any aspiration or capability to assume the mantle of global leadership—or in most cases even regional leadership. Russia is a declining power that is using the fissures in the Western alliance and its own asymmetrical cyber and paramilitary capabilities to sow limited chaos in Western political systems and to block former Soviet states from consolidating their security and economic relationships with NATO. China, like rising powers throughout history, is free-riding on American leadership globally while engaging in limited revisionism regionally. Beijing will do what it can to assert its control over the East and South China Seas, but unlike Russia has a great stake in the current international economic order and limited appetite for direct confrontation with the United States. Iran remains a revolutionary regime with historic irredentist aspirations and the potential to destabilize friendly Gulf states that have dissatisfied Shi'a populations within, but the growing threat Iran is posing despite the recent nuclear agreement is also breaking down barriers between erstwhile adversaries in the region, including the Gulf states and Israel. Indeed, all of these potential regional revisionists—particularly China—face the risk of increased counterbalancing and even new collective security arrangements if their irredentist behavior increases. Finally, North Korea, though it poses a significantly higher material threat with nuclear weapons, is entirely focused on regime survival and has little ability to dictate the terms of Northeast Asia's future.

More broadly, the Western Hemisphere faces no serious hegemonic aspirant other than possibly Brazil (a stretch), and though the region still suffers from poor democratic governance in some countries, it is generally a net exporter of security and prosperity in contrast to its past. On the whole, CNN journalist Fareed Zakaria's hypothesis that the United States will benefit from the "rise of the rest" remains viable.

Nevertheless, the growing defense spending, asymmetrical capabilities, and tolerance for risk by potential regional challengers in Asia, Europe, and the Gulf have raised the level of uncertainty about American leadership globally. In none of these regions are allies stepping up sufficiently in response to coercive moves, nor do key allies see the United States as sufficiently focused on deterrence in their own near abroad. Yet the revisionist powers in each region are cooperating with each other only superficially because they all see potential existential threats from each other: Iranian support for Islamic revolutions could destabilize both China and Russia's Islamic minorities; China's growth could overwhelm Russia's Far East; Russia's ideological war with the United States could entrap China in conflicts it does not need; and only Iran sees benefit in North Korea's nuclear breakout. No such mutual threat perception exists among or between the world's leading democratic nations. The problem is that there is no coherent geopolitical concept of "the West" any longer in Washington, London, or Berlin. The power of the democratic nations to deal with regional revisionism is still less than the sum of the parts. For example, Europe often undermines U.S. allies in the Pacific by eschewing any significant role in responding to Chinese coercion in East Asia, while Japan's ambitious pitch to woo Russia from China in the Far East has the potential to undermine strategies of the trans-Atlantic alliance.

One dimension of this problem is the increasingly contested expansion of democratic norms and rule of law in all regions. In the years just before and after the end of the Cold War, democratic governments emerged across East Asia and Eastern Europe—from Korea and Indonesia to Poland and Ukraine. Polls taken in Asia today indicate that people are far more likely to identify with democratic norms and rule of law than the so-called Beijing consensus of authoritarian development. Yet authoritarianism is returning in Russia, China, Turkey, Hungary, Cambodia, Thailand, the Philippines, and scores of other countries. Fearful of "colored revolutions," Russia and China began comparing notes at the Shanghai Cooperation Organization 10 years ago on how to close civil society space and intimidate or silence political opponents and the press. Their basic blueprint has been used with success ever since. Freedom House reports the lowest level of press freedom in 12 years. Meanwhile, spending by the United States and Europe on assistance for governance and democracy abroad has dropped since 2009 while public opinion surveys show that Americans have deemphasized support for democracy as a foreign policy priority over the same period. In a 2014 survey of elite opinion, CSIS found that American experts were second only to Chinese experts in their skepticism about democracy and human rights promotion in Asia, even though support for those objectives went up in the rest of the region. These trends may reflect American frustration with the democratic process at home and the impact of the wars in the Middle East, but they also echo the decreasing emphasis of democratic norms by leaders in the United States and Europe.

In the postwar period, the Bretton Woods system, and later the EU, the G-5, and the G-7 reinforced support for open societies and economies. This institutional architecture had to expand and "democratize" itself with the rise of the BRICS and the 2008 financial crisis, most notably with the establishment of the G-20. The G-20 played a critical role in rebuilding an international consensus against protectionism in the midst of the financial crisis, but the grouping has proven too large and ideologically diverse to set a proactive global economic agenda the way the G-7 had. In Europe the EU seemed poised to establish a Europe whole and free, but Brexit demonstrated the weak popular foundations of the European experiment, including in continental Europe where polls suggest a British-style plebiscite might also result in an "exit" result. Asia's explosion of postwar institutions, though less ambitious, has also hit diminishing returns because of political diversity and the return of earlier geopolitical rivalries. CSIS elite surveys in Asia 2009 found little confidence that the alphabet soup of multilateral meetings in the region (ARF, APEC, EAS, etc.) would prove useful in an actual crisis, and a follow-up survey in 2014 showed growing pessimism about the growth of multilateralism in the region. The EU and the Association of Southeast Asian Nations (ASEAN) simultaneously revealed their Achilles' heels in July 2016 when China was able to buy off Cambodia, Greece, Hungary, and Slovenia and thus block consensus in both Europe and Asia in support of the UN Convention on the Law of the Sea (UNCLOS) arbitration panel's favorable ruling for the Philippines. It was disturbing to see that the weakest link could cripple both regional organizations' ability to stand up to revisionist behavior. Meanwhile, new institutions are emerging that appear to challenge the established multilateral organizations. China's Asian Infrastructure Investment Bank (AIIB) appeared one such example when it was announced in 2014.

Yet the revisionist challenge to existing international and regional institutions should not be overstated. China or Russia may be able to blunt geopolitical action by the EU or ASEAN by picking off individual states, but geopolitical action has always depended more on NATO or the U.S. alliance system in Asia in the first place. Moreover, the EU, and to a lesser extent, ASEAN, continue to define the terms of entry into European and Asian regionalism in ways that potential revisionist powers cannot. In addition, there is no organizational alternative to the EU in Europe while in Asia the closest thing to a non-U.S. regional grouping is the Regional Comprehensive Economic Partnership (RCEP), but RCEP includes U.S.

allies like Japan, Korea, and Australia and is still far behind the trans-Pacific TPP process in terms of rule-making and liberalization. Indeed, both RCEP and TPP are understood by the United States and China as falling under a broader inclusive integration effort agreed to at APEC in 2007. Similarly, China's AIIB may look and operate differently from the World Bank or Asian Development Bank, but it is now closely cooperating with both institutions.

The traditional postwar foundations of the U.S.-led international order are thus all under some duress, but far from crumbling. That then leads to the new sources of entropy in the international system that were never conceived when the postwar order was being constructed: namely, the global threats that emanate from globalization and nonstate actors. Interestingly, the Bush and Obama administrations both argued in their first National Security Strategy documents that global challenges could unite geopolitical rivals and stabilize international order. For Bush, of course, it was the common front against terrorism, and for Obama it was cooperation on the threat of climate change. Both administrations were correct in part. Great power relations did stabilize somewhat because of the global war on terror, while one of the few positive areas of cooperation in U.S.-China relations today is in the area of climate change. The Bush administration also built greater international cooperation and trust around the international cooperation to meet the avian influenza threat, and the Obama administration rallied international support to deal with the Zika virus. At the same time, it is clearly not the case that cooperation on global challenges fundamentally changed geopolitics as the current tensions in U.S.-China relations demonstrate. To date these global challenges have neither weakened nor strengthened the foundations of the U.S. international order in any significant way. On the other hand, there could be a catastrophic impact on global order should climate change cause fights for scarce water resources or destabilize whole states—or should animal-to-human transmission of a deadly virus force the closure of international flights and trade in the event of an unprecedented international pandemic. Technology also accelerates the impacts of globalization as nuclear and especially biological weapons become more accessible, while the Internet of things and thus the global economy itself becomes more vulnerable to cyber attack.

What is one to think of global order given these new scenarios? It would not be accurate to say that the foundations of the U.S.-led global order are crumbling as a result of globalization and technology. These are still largely hypothetical scenarios after all, despite the reality of the technology that could drive them. Indeed, information technology could accelerate change in other directions as well. For example, 3-D printing could reconcentrate economic competitiveness around the United States, and social media penetration could ultimately tip the scales in favor of freedom even if authoritarian governments have skillfully used the Internet to create an impasse for now.

Yet the conclusion for policymakers and strategists should be the same either way. The foundations of the neoliberal order are not crumbling, but they have been shaken from within and without, and they could be destroyed in the most cataclysmic scenarios resulting from globalization and diffusion of advanced technologies. The answer is to begin reinforcing resilience and strengthening from within. If the core is American capacity and willpower, there is still much to work with, but it will require rebuilding the case for international leadership in the wake of this very damaging election. The next concentric circle is the U.S. network of bilateral and regional alliances, bound by common interests and values. This second ring must be reinforced with greater jointness, interoperability, and common purpose within and among U.S. alliances, including renewed efforts at defense modernization, trade liberalization, and collective global support for democratic rules and norms. The ability to dissuade revisionism by nondemocratic powers will in turn depend on solidarity within what was once known as the "West"—but now includes many more democratic partners in the Far East. Ultimately, the U.S.-led regional order will depend on sharing power with a rising China and India—just as it depended on sharing power with a rising Japan and Germany in the twentieth century. But strengthening the core of the international system must come before compromises are made to the rules and norms that make that system function.

Ultimately, it will depend on leadership. When we needed Truman, Adenauer, and Yoshida, we had them. When we needed Reagan, Thatcher, Kohl, and Nakasone, we had them once again. We now need leaders who can harness their citizens to defend and expand freedom and prosperity, yet liberal democracies are serving up a disappointing mix of transactional, populist, and ineffective heads of state. History suggests that there is nothing permanent about the nature of leadership, though. New leadership may emerge precisely because the liberal democracies have something fundamental their citizens will want them to defend. Making that point is the first task of the next generation of leaders we need.

3. WHAT GLOBAL ECONOMIC RISKS DO WE FACE?

A conversation with Heather A. Conley,
Matthew P. Goodman, and Scott Miller

Craig Cohen and Josiane Gabel: *Eight years after the financial crisis, let's take stock of where we stand. How are the economies in the developed West, emerging Asia, and other parts of the world performing? How do we expect them to perform over the next few years?*

Matthew P. Goodman: The global economy is still not in a good place. Global GDP growth has disappointed relative to precrisis trends, averaging just above 3 percent per year since 2008. Even this modest level of growth has required an explosion of debt: the global debt-to-GDP ratio has risen almost 10 percentage points since the crisis. Trade growth, which used to comfortably outpace GDP growth before the crisis, has weakened significantly to just above 2 percent per year. Even in the United States, where job growth has been relatively robust, wages have only just passed their 1996 level.

All of this is taking place against a backdrop of enormous political uncertainty and rapid technological change. Either of these could bring further disruption. It's no surprise that business investment has been stubbornly subdued across the globe.

Scott Miller: Most forecasters estimate global growth will be stuck at around 3 percent to 3.5 percent, with the United States delivering the same old 2 percent real growth for 2017 and 2018. Essentially, forecasts tell us to "embrace the boredom." Absent the capacity for a big dose of monetary or fiscal stimulus, slow growth is certainly better than none at all.

Goodman: Growth in emerging markets will be more robust, but it is neither strong nor likely to be sustainable. China is continuing its structural slowdown. Even if India maintains growth in the 7 percent range, no single country can drive regional growth.

Heather A. Conley: Europe continues to be plagued by high levels of debt, weak growth, and a very fragile banking sector, which grows ever weaker from negative interest rates and the weight of nonperforming loans. Five Eurozone countries' debt-to-GDP ratio exceeded 105 percent at the end of 2015. Surprises could throw Europe's "muddle through" strategy off track, but we should also prepare for surprises with unanticipated upsides. For now, the economic impact of Brexit has not followed the predicted path of economic Armageddon.

Cohen and Gabel: *Looking at the current global economic landscape, what do you think are some of the key risks that policymakers need to be alert to? Could we see another downturn on par with what we saw in 2008? What about the reverse—do you see any underappreciated strengths? And what should policymakers be doing about all of this?*

Goodman: The good news is that the major economies have done a lot to address the vulnerabilities in the global financial system that produced the last crisis. But even as greater resilience has lowered the probability of a 2008-style financial crisis, it would be hard to argue the risks are gone.

One risk is macroeconomic policy error. The U.S. recovery is still not especially strong, and the Federal Reserve should be wary of raising interest rates too quickly. In Europe and Japan, leaders should avoid the temptation to cut government spending too soon.

There are also looming financial risks. Europe needs to deal with a banking sector that is still too weak to withstand an external shock, as we saw when Italian banks wobbled after the Brexit vote. China needs to address mounting corporate debt and industrial overcapacity to avoid its own "lost decade."

More difficult for policymakers, but no less necessary, will be addressing structural constraints that both inhibit growth today and could lead to a crisis down the road.

Conley: In Europe, the risks are plenty. There are the anemic French and Italian economies, a banking sector too closely linked to government, high sovereign debt, high unemployment especially among youth, a looming demographic crisis, and increasingly protectionist and nationalistic instincts.

But Europe also has strengths that are underappreciated. The export-driven German economy continues to perform well, as does the British economy, Brexit notwithstanding. Europe has strong democratic institutions and predictable legal systems, globally desirable goods and services, a highly educated workforce, developed infrastructure, and a welcoming investment climate. This is why both American and Chinese firms find Europe so attractive as an economic destination despite its current economic woes.

Miller: The U.S. and other advanced economies face more downside risks than upside at this point in the business cycle. The current U.S. expansion is 90 months old, longer than the post-WWII average of 56 months, and price inflation is headed up slowly. Interest rates remain extraordinarily low worldwide, but are unlikely to stay that way. The end of "free money"—whether it is a result of markets or the action of central banks—is a likely source of instability. Sovereign debt loads have increased dramatically since 2008, and debt service obligations will crowd out other fiscal measures.

Here in the United States, tax reform could provide incentives for stronger capital formation and productivity growth, which have disappointed since the 2008 recession. Absent real financial leadership, though, status quo politics will likely deliver no better than status quo growth.

Cohen and Gabel: *Europe was hit particularly hard in 2008. What are its prospects for recovery? There's no denying that its economic woes are having political implications. Can you give us a sense of how stagnant growth might lead to increased populism and nationalism, and how this* *might play out in elections across Europe and in the broader effort to hold Europe together post-Brexit?*

Conley: Despite signs of recovery, the perception in Europe remains that the economy is stagnant. This creates palpable anxiety that wreaks political and economic havoc. To give you a sense of the anxiety, the European Central Bank has maintained interest rates near zero, but instead of encouraging spending, the net savings rate of households and businesses actually rose by 40 percent!

Juxtapose this with the fact that three-fourths of Eurozone economies will have national elections or referendums between now and the end of 2017. When anxiety meets popular will, the results can be unpredictable to say the least. This is what happened with Brexit, what happened with our elections, what is happening at present with the political chaos in Italy, and what could occur in 2017 with elections in France and Germany.

Miller: It is a destabilizing brew—slow growth and high unemployment, with little room for additional monetary or fiscal stimulus.

Goodman: It is a fragile moment right now in Europe. France and Spain are recovering, but both still face high unemployment. The UK faces great uncertainty depending on whether we see a "hard" or "soft" Brexit. The biggest obstacle to recovery in Europe is probably Germany, even though it continues to enjoy steady growth and rising wages. There will be limits to Europe's recovery so long as Berlin refuses to use more expansionary fiscal policy. But it has its own politics to worry about.

Cohen and Gabel: *Populist forces around the world are taking aim at trade as being skewed toward big business and fostering inequality. What is the best chance for rescuing a trade agenda and avoiding tariff wars in the years ahead? What should the G7 be doing?*

Miller: Venture capitalist and Trump supporter Peter Thiel summed it up in a recent speech at the National Press Club: "No matter what happens this election, what Trump represents isn't crazy and it's not going away." Mainly, the protectionist backlash evidences a failure of political leadership. But because the

forces behind the current turbulence are principally technological, it's important for leaders to recognize that policies that
"worked" in a different environment may not be effective in the
future. Technology, not policy, is the prime mover behind
today's intensified intercountry competitiveness, and yester-
day's trade or currency deals with advanced economies will
not suffice.

The sliver of "good news" is that most Americans seem to
understand that times have changed. Polls show steady support
for trade and trade agreements despite harsh campaign rhetoric. Without question, arriving at new policies suited for a
new reality will take time and energy. In the meantime, elected
officials in the G7 and elsewhere should work to avoid "vandalism"
to the current structure while accelerating an appreciation of
how the "new" economy really works and how to address those
new challenges with people, ideas, and effort.

Goodman: Trade has become a scapegoat for an array of grievances relating to rapid changes in the economy and society.
Like technological progress, more open trade brings broad
and substantial benefits to an economy. However, it is also true
that trade causes real disruption to some workers and companies. Governments have not done a good enough job on either
side of this story: explaining the benefits of trade or addressing
its adjustment costs.

Rebuilding support for trade and trade agreements begins
with making greater investments in the domestic underpinnings
of a strong and competitive economy, including infrastructure,
education and training, and innovation. More assistance for
workers disrupted by economic change—whether caused by trade
or technological progress—is also needed.

Conley: One of the most vocal public expressions of European
anxiety and uncertainty is a rising revolt against free trade, a
catchall issue for the disruptive nature of globalization. Pop-
ulists have effectively channeled this fear and anxiety and
sought to eliminate any form of compromise between international trade and national economic policies. As leaders such as

France's far-right Marine Le Pen have stated: Are you a patriot or a globalist? According to Ms. Le Pen and other nationalists of her ilk, you cannot be both. G7 nations must create the policy space where "patriots" and "globalists" can claim success, which would mean that patriotism is redefined as a nation's ability to become more successful in a globalized economy and globalists alter how they conduct business and negotiate trade agreements to become more responsive to national and regional demands and developments. Both sides must change how they have done business for the past 20 years and find a new middle ground, yet both sides appear to be digging their trenches ever deeper in preparation for a battle of attrition.

Cohen and Gabel: *How much does U.S. leadership matter? What would you say to someone who says, "The U.S. president has little effect over the global economy, European politics, or populist forces around the world"?*

Goodman: The United States remains an "indispensable nation" in global economic affairs. Our position as the world's largest market and a leading source of technology and capital gives us unparalleled leverage in encouraging pro-growth policies and championing an open, rules-based global economic order. You can see this at play in G20 meetings, where most countries play a passive role and wait for the United States to propose a course of action. Of course Washington doesn't always get what it wants, and needs support to solve most global economic challenges, but without U.S. leadership the global economic order would be far less stable, predictable, and successful than it has been for the past 75 years.

Miller: The wave of "globalization" that began in the late 1980s was initiated by U.S. technological, political, and military leadership. Its expansion was supported by an economic architecture created and sustained by the United States and key allies. Millions were lifted out of poverty, yet no economy benefited more than our own, with its relative openness, strong institutions, and adaptive, entrepreneurial people. Globalization has now entered a new phase, but I am confident that, if anyone can figure out how to make it work in a mutually beneficial manner, it is the American people, driven by their ingenuity, sense of fair play, and drive to make things better.

Conley: As the largest Western economy, the United States must lead the way to regaining lost confidence. A strong American economy will strengthen Europe's economy. When political paralysis in the United States finally gives way, this will send a positive and powerful message to other advanced countries that they can overcome their crises. Western confidence can be restored, but for the moment, populism and anxiety are in the ascendancy and Western confidence is in retreat.

4. WILL RUSSIA CONTINUE TO PLAY THE ROLE OF SPOILER?

Olga Oliker

U.S. relations with Russia have been in a tailspin for almost three years. Moscow's decision in early 2014 to annex Crimea and use military force there and in Eastern Ukraine put a seeming end to almost a quarter century of Western efforts to engage and integrate Russia. In their place has come a spiral of tension and a new conventional wisdom that whatever the path forward, the United States and its allies are in for a long, tough ride with the Russians.

In the wake of the election of Donald Trump to the presidency of the United States, however, not a few have asked if this is still the case. The president-elect has made a point of his desire to mend fences with Russian president Vladimir Putin. This has led to speculation, in Russia and the West, that the incoming administration will seek some sort of deal with the Kremlin, ending the standoff and setting the stage for a categorically new relationship.

I would caution the next administration to move carefully on this front. This is not because better relations with Russia are a bad idea. To the contrary, both countries have a lot to gain from cooperation, and much to lose from conflict, rhetorical and real. However, Donald Trump will be the third of as many U.S. presidents that have begun their tenure pledging a new, more collaborative, way forward with Vladimir Putin's Russia. There are reasons that this has repeatedly proven more difficult than it seemed.

To define policy toward Russia, it helps to consider Russia's perspective. The Kremlin has a foreign policy explicitly centered on prestige, and it seeks to gain that prestige by "standing up" to Washington. This derives in part from a consistently zero-sum view of the world: for Moscow to be strong, it must be strong in comparison to others. The United States, which emerged from the Cold War as the world's sole superpower, is a natural yardstick. Moreover, the Kremlin sees the United States as having prosecuted a concerted policy of punishing and weakening Russia. Today, in its view, Russia has finally grown strong enough to push back. As a result, and over the last three years especially, one of Moscow's goals has been to demonstrate that Russia, too, can do the sorts of things the United States does (including foreign interference), and that it can keep the United States from always getting what it wants. In practice, this has meant that Russia has sought not only to advance its own, specific goals. It has also looked for opportunities to challenge U.S. policies and leadership, and to present a Cold War–like juxtaposition between the two countries. Washington, meanwhile, with its global goals and interests, has tended to notice Russian positions and concerns only when the Russians force the point. It has therefore viewed many of Russia's policies and actions as part of a strategy of spoilerism.

Spoilerism or not, Russian actions have effects. While few doubted Moscow's ability to wreak chaos in Ukraine, Russia's military involvement in Syria surprised many by making a real difference: although it did not bring the country any closer to peace, it has decisively bolstered the Assad regime and changed facts on the ground. In Europe, while Russia's Ukraine operation may now appear to be something of a morass, its second-order implications have the potential to shift long-standing continental dynamics. If Russia was not, initially, in any doubt about NATO's alliance commitments and the EU's institutional strength, now, between populist political movements and very public soul-searching about Europe's future, Moscow may well feel that it has real openings to challenge European and Western unity and its institutions. Evidence of Russian interference in a range of domestic political processes—from an attempted coup in Macedonia to the release of hacked e-mails from

America's Democratic Party leadership in the midst of our election—has fostered distrust and frustration. Some Westerners see Russian fingerprints in every setback. Others ignore the phenomenon entirely. But the lesson for Russia is that this sort of thing can work, and that it may make Russia look more powerful and capable than it actually is.

Meanwhile, Russia is also facing a continuing economic recession at home, one rooted less in the sanctions imposed on it in the wake of its actions in Ukraine, and more in the combination of low oil prices and failure to carry out structural reforms when the economy was stronger. To date, the Kremlin has been able to blame the bulk of these problems on the United States and its European allies, muting (or at least refocusing) domestic discontent. This suggests that for Moscow, a better relationship with Washington is a mixed blessing: Russia is seeing a strategy of brinksmanship and escalation bear fruit in attaining a range of goals, and may have reason to think that more is possible. If fences are mended with the United States, at least some of this will have to be curtailed.

In this environment, if the Trump administration seeks deals, it must remain aware of several things. First among them is that it is not the coming to power of a new U.S. president that makes deals possible. Deals have been on the table all along: the problem was that Russia wanted them on its own terms only. Sanctions could have been (and still can be) lifted if Russia was willing to make progress on its commitments under the Minsk II agreement, meant to settle the Ukraine crisis. Russia could have had cooperation in Syria if it was, well, willing to actually cooperate, rather than do its utmost to ensure an Assad victory in Aleppo. So given a situation where Russia actually benefits from the status quo, and is facing a U.S. administration that seeks better relations, Russia is likely to try to get the same sorts of deals it has sought all along: ones that are all about U.S. concessions. At a minimum, these might include acceptance of the status quo in Ukraine, lifting of sanctions, and support for Assad in Syria. More maximally, Russia may seek pledges of no NATO membership for Ukraine (and other post-Soviet countries) and limitations on the U.S. and NATO role (and force posture) in Europe. It may want pledges of noninterference (as defined by Moscow) in Russia's internal politics and those of its neighbors. Whatever the concessions, if all that the United States gets in exchange is a deal, then it is a bad deal. This is not just because these concessions will undermine European trust and security and do nothing to stabilize Syria. It is a bad deal because, as noted above, Russia views international relations as a zero-sum game, and Washington as its primary adversary. This means that when the United States takes a step back, Russia sees weakness. When it takes a step forward, Moscow sees threat. This security dilemma will not change because Donald Trump takes office.

Moreover, a bad deal will eventually be recognized as such. European responses to Washington selling out its allies will hurt the United States as well as the continent. Meanwhile, a Russia fresh from U.S. concessions while still dealing with substantial challenges at home will seek, and expect, more. Frustration by either or both parties will then almost certainly lead to a relationship even worse than the current one (and without the Western unity that has been so crucial over the last three years, and, indeed, for decades). Expect, in this case, to see even more Russian interference in other states' domestic politics. Expect arms races and escalating military brinksmanship. Expect an increased risk of conflict, with all the dangers that implies.

None of this is meant to argue that the United States should avoid deals. It simply means that any deals struck with Russia must recognize and manage the security dilemma. This means that they must include clear gains for the United States, ones that are evident not just to the White House, but also to the Kremlin. Arrangements that advance security goals for allies and partners, with their full involvement, will also help ensure U.S. and Russian security. Progress in arms control and nonproliferation; serious, multilateral engagement on Europe's security future; and a way forward in Syria that includes sustainable reconstruction could all be pursued to positive effect. The Trump administration may have less interest in and standing to pressure Russia on human rights, but it will do no one, including itself, any favors by giving up Washington's prerogative to hold other states accountable. But if a deal for its own sake is insufficient, unsustainable, and dangerous, agreements that genuinely benefit both parties are not only possible, but likely to be critical if we are to avoid further cycles of hostility.

5. HOW SHOULD WE VIEW CHINA'S RISE?

A conversation with Christopher K. Johnson, Victor Cha, and Amy Searight

Craig Cohen and Josiane Gabel: *It is evident that China's rise will continue to dominate the geopolitics of Asia. How do the Chinese view this? Do its neighbors view it as inevitable, benign, or concerning? Where is there greatest convergence of Chinese views with that of its neighbors, and where is the greatest divergence?*

Christopher K. Johnson: If China's economic, military, and geopolitical influence continues to rise at even a modest pace during the next few decades, the world will witness the largest shift in the global distribution of power since the rise of the United States in the late nineteenth and early twentieth centuries. And, if China in the next 10 to 15 years surpasses the United States as the world's largest economy, it will mark the first time in centuries that the world's economic leader will be non-English speaking, non-Western, and nondemocratic.

Of course, these are some pretty big ifs. China's leaders will have to demonstrate sufficient foresight and flexibility to respond to immediate tactical concerns while always staying mindful of their geostrategic long game. They will have to prove that China's political and economic rise will be as sustainable over the next 30 years as it has been over the last third of a century, even though the task they are confronting now, as highlighted by the economy's present struggles with maintaining lift, arguably is much more complex than that faced by their predecessors.

They will have to craft a workable strategic framework for channeling the country's growing wealth and power in a way that facilitates China's return to the dominant position in East Asia without sparking conflict with their neighbors or, more importantly, with the United States. And, more fundamentally, they must find an answer to the nagging question of what type of great power China wants to be in terms of whether or not to adhere to long-established global rules of the game that they had no hand in shaping. How China manages the tricky balance between the interests that encourage it to be a status quo power and the instinct to be a more disruptive one will largely determine how it interacts with its regional neighbors going forward.

Amy Searight: China's neighbors in Southeast Asia view China's rise as inevitable and also indispensable to their own economic prosperity. China has been the engine of economic growth in the region for decades, and Southeast Asian countries have sought to hitch their wagons to China's dynamism, embracing the growing trade and investment linkages that have transformed the region into a growing web of regional production networks. The rise of manufacturing jobs and overall economic growth has lifted a vast number of Southeast Asians out of poverty and created bright economic prospects for many of these countries.

At the same time, however, China's growing assertiveness and coercion in the maritime domain and on the diplomatic front are creating great anxiety in the region and wariness over China's regional strategic ambitions. China's self-declared "peaceful rise" is looking a lot less benign to its neighbors as it flexes its muscles in the South China Sea and seeks to divide ASEAN on key issues. In response, many ASEAN countries are seeking to balance their economic dependence on China with stronger security ties with the United States along with other regional powers, like Japan, India, and Australia.

Victor Cha: I think if you poll the region's elites (as CSIS has done), two observations become clear. First, every country in the region acknowledges that China will be the dominant power in the region over the next 10 years. However, those same countries poll very differently when it comes to the question of how comfortable they are with China as the dominant power. Indeed, even Chinese are uncomfortable with this thought. For this reason, many of the countries polled felt the U.S. role as a stabilizer and its political leadership was critical to their own sense of security.

The greatest area of convergence, I think, is on regional economic integration. Asia for so long has been economically less cohesive as a community. The 1997–1998 Asian financial crisis was a real wake-up call, and we have seen increasing integration in terms of trade and investment since then. The greatest area of divergence will be on manifestations of China's growth that impinge on the sovereignty of others, as we are seeing in the South China Sea.

Cohen and Gabel: *There is an assumption among some in Washington that the Chinese will become more assertive as their capabilities increase and Beijing increasingly defines its defensive interests in broader terms. Do you agree with this? Is there a possibility they will use their increased leverage in common purpose with the United States on certain issues?*

Johnson: I am ceaselessly surprised by how much handwringing goes on in Washington on this topic. Of course China will be more active abroad as its expanding global interests—whether in terms of energy security, trade and investment, or a growing inclination from the international community to seek Beijing's participation in tackling the many challenges that confront the world—pull China in that direction. This is an entirely natural development and should be expected and not feared.

As to how a growing Chinese global role impacts U.S.-China relations, the broad parameters of the policy challenge for Washington remain the same: encouraging China's integration into the rules-based global order while hedging against Chinese behavior that might undermine it. The difficulty, in my mind, is that the complexity of the task facing American policymakers is growing in light of the increasingly multidimensional character of the bilateral relationship at the same time the number of foreign policy issues vying for their attention also is rising.

As such, my sense is that the incoming Trump administration needs to take a hard look at how it wants to approach U.S.-China ties, with a particular focus on the basic mechanics of how we engage in light of President Xi Jinping's rewiring of policy formulation and execution in China. This is especially necessary given that even areas that historically have been clear points of bilateral convergence—such as the economic and trade relationship—are trending toward greater competition.

Searight: It is only natural for a rising power like China with growing regional and global equities to define its interests more broadly and engage more actively in defense, diplomacy, and power projection. China's maritime military modernization is a case in point. As China's global trade and resource dependence has expanded, it has a growing interest in building the capability to protect critical trade routes without reliance on the U.S. Navy.

In recent years China has invested heavily in its navy and transformed it from a coastal force into a blue water navy, capable of far-reaching operations across oceans. China has used its new naval capabilities to build influence in the region and beyond, and to contribute to global maritime security efforts, most notably its regular contributions to international counter-piracy operations in the Horn of Africa since 2008. China's navy has also become more active in humanitarian missions, deploying its hospital ship *Peace Ark* annually for longer duration and great distances. Counter-piracy and humanitarian assistance are two areas where the United States and China already cooperate through naval exchanges and exercises, and there are other areas of potential cooperation as well, such as maritime safety and risk reduction. More broadly, when the interests of the United States and China align, we can expect to see expanded military-to-military cooperation. On the other hand, where interests diverge, such as U.S. Freedom of Navigation Operations (FONOPs) in the South China Sea, we can expect to see growing friction.

Cha: I do think there is a linear calculation in most of Washington about Chinese power and Chinese intentions. This is not because China is communist, but because China is behaving as most great powers do historically when they rise. So, there will be natural friction, competition that will emerge between the rising power and the hegemon (United States) in the coming two decades. The key for policymakers is to ensure that this competition, which can sometimes be healthy in terms of spurring innovation, does not spiral into military conflict. The greatest areas of most common purpose between a rising China and the United States may be on global issues like climate change, rather than issues in the region.

Cohen and Gabel: *What do you think the Chinese long game is in the South China Sea, and what more, if anything, could the United States be doing to preserve freedom of navigation over time?*

Searight: As China has taken increasingly assertive actions in the South China Sea—building up artificial islands and turning them into military outposts, threatening its neighbors and harassing U.S. vessels—it has become pretty clear that China's long-run ambition is to control the South China Sea.

Control over this critical waterway and its land features would secure the natural resources for China's exclusive use and would provide security for maritime approaches to China, enabling it to deny access to enemy forces in the event of a conflict. It would also go a long way to restoring a Sinocentric regional order that features prominently in China's popular imagination, and would thus help maintain the legitimacy of the Chinese Communist Party.

Although China is unlikely to impede freedom of navigation for international commerce during peacetime, its challenges to military freedom of navigation and overflight, and its attempts to exercise jurisdiction over rival claimants in disputed areas, will continue and probably increase as its capabilities grow.

Current U.S. policies, consisting of routine presence operations as well as operational assertions under the Freedom of Navigation Program, are probably sufficient to preserve U.S. freedom of navigation during peacetime. The key is to maintain consistency and demonstrate resolve. FONOPs, for example, should be conducted like clockwork, challenging excessive claims of both China and other claimants. FONOPs should not be ratcheted up or down according to political considerations, but should be used to establish a baseline communication of the United States' opposition to excessive maritime claims and its resolve to fully exercise its maritime rights and freedoms.

Preserving U.S. freedom of navigation in the South China Sea during a conflict will become increasingly difficult as Chinese military capabilities grow. Maintaining deterrence by introducing advanced U.S. capabilities, developing new operational concepts, and enhancing U.S. forward presence through a more distributed, resilient, and sustainable force posture will be important to prevent conflict and avoid a costly struggle to regain access to the South China Sea.

Cha: A scholar recently wrote that the South China Sea is to China what the Caribbean was to the young United States a couple of centuries ago. It was our strategic imperative to remove all European powers from nearby waters. Perhaps that is what China is thinking in terms of the South China Sea. But those were different times. The dollar value of trade that flows through these waters is immense. And countries in the region are not comfortable with China's harassing vessels in these waters or declaring an Air Defense Identification Zone (ADIZ).

The dilemma for the United States is how to deter further Chinese land reclamation and building when these reefs, rocks, and islets cannot be conceived of as a core U.S. national security interest. Building the capacity of other smaller countries in the region is important, but perhaps most important is for China and the region to see the United States as "present" in the region. This means a regular tempo of naval activity and FONOPs but without necessarily a lot of pomp and circumstance. Quietly but deliberately showing the U.S. Navy's reach is about the best way to convey this.

Johnson: I'm glad you asked about China's long game. So often, it is far too easy for us to get caught up in some new development on a particular island or land feature and lose sight of the fact that all of these developments should be understood against the backdrop of an integrated maritime strategy that China has been unambiguously signaling it would undertake since the 2012 18th Party Congress.

China's turn to a more robust assertion of its claims in the South China Sea seems motivated by two key drivers, one tactical, and the other more strategic. On the tactical side, Beijing's activism reflects its assessment that it lost substantial ground to its rival claimants during its long (1996–2008) entanglement in managing heightened tensions across the Taiwan Strait. China's irritation at being outmaneuvered by its smaller, far less powerful competitors, coupled with a growing sense of confidence in its capacity to effect meaningful change, combined to unleash the robust pushback that has characterized China's actions for the last several—and particularly the last few—years.

More broadly, China's approach reflects its interest in developing more maritime strategic depth on its periphery as its interests expand well beyond its shores. In effect, China sees its activities in the South China Sea as contributing to its efforts to signal its regional neighbors, and the United States, that its forces intend to operate at times of their choosing, and perhaps, at times, with impunity, out to the second island chain and beyond into the Western Pacific.

Cohen and Gabel: *Is China a reliable ally in our desire to encourage a more predictable and stable North Korea? What leverage do they really hold over Pyongyang, and under what circumstances would they be willing to use it?*

Cha: By any metric China's future on the Korean peninsula is with the South and not the North. China does about 200 times more economic business with the South than the North per annum. While China has many political and economic benefits to reap from its relationship with an advanced industrialized democracy in Seoul, it throws money down a black hole in its assistance to the mercurial Kim regime. Hope springs eternal that China will choose to cut the albatross off its neck, but the world has been disappointed each time. We should still continue to press, persuade, and promote China to take a more responsible position in its relations with North Korea, but we should not at the same time subcontract the policy over a core threat to U.S. national security to a great power competitor.

Johnson: It would be wrong to think of China as an ally on managing North Korea. China can be a partner, and quite an effective one, with the United States in the few areas where our interests on the Peninsula align, but the fact remains that, while China has absolute leverage over the North in the form of food, energy, and other types of aid, Beijing remains absolutely unwilling to use it.

Chinese fears of a regime collapse that precipitates a flood of refugees into northeast China and arguably outdated notions regarding the strategic value of North Korea as a "buffer zone" against U.S. forces in the South seem to be preventing the Politburo from fully grasping how Pyongyang's advances in its nuclear and ballistic missile programs are dramatically altering the U.S. strategic imperative to get the North to change course.

In fairness, the Chinese leadership's reluctance to press its erstwhile ally probably stems in part from what seems to be its substantially diminished insight into what is actually happening inside the Kim regime, increasing Beijing's risk avoidance when it comes to rattling the North Korean leader's cage.

As such, Washington is likely to have to rely on more unilateral measures to move the dial on the North Korean nuclear issue.

Cohen and Gabel: *How do you think Xi would like to be remembered—what are the legacy issues for him? Do you think his view of "U.S. leadership" is compatible with our own?*

Johnson: President Xi has been fairly explicit in terms of setting out his primary goals for his leadership tenure. Concepts such as the "Chinese dream," "the great rejuvenation of the Chinese nation," and the "twin centenary goals" may all sound like vapid Marxist sloganeering to a Western ear, but given that this is the lexicon in which Xi chooses to communicate with his Politburo colleagues, we dismiss it at our peril.

Xi's innovation with these concepts is his argument that the encapsulation of all of the foundational elements of Chinese statecraft lies in the realization of a future wherein the PRC by 2049 intends to restore itself to a regional position of primacy. Unlike the policy platforms of Western political parties where it is understood that few of the stated goals ultimately will be realized, the Chinese Communist Party views its analogous pronouncements as strategic benchmarks that must be achieved to promote and sustain the legitimacy of continued one-party rule. As such, we can expect Xi to be willing to spend political capital, both domestically and abroad, in seeking to attain them.

As to the issue of "U.S. leadership," whether in the region or globally, Xi sees U.S. power as a lesser constraint on China's exercise of its influence—both benign and coercive—than earlier leaders. In fact, ties with the United States, while still meriting pride of place in the hierarchy of Beijing's foreign relationships, seem less of a preoccupation for Xi than for his predecessors. This is not to suggest that he is not eager for stable and healthy U.S.-China ties. Rather, Xi seems to prefer a more casual approach to the relationship that lacks the eagerness and rapt attention that characterized the policies of Hu Jintao and Jiang Zemin. This less awestruck view of U.S. power con-

tributes to Xi's greater tolerance for risk and has the important side effect of imbuing Xi with greater confidence to more
deliberately court China's other important foreign partners
rather than pursuing a single-minded focus on the United
States.

6. CAN AMERICA STILL RELY ON ITS ALLIES?

Andrew Shearer

Alliances are costly, in treasure and potentially in blood. Over more than half a century, the United States has invested trillions of dollars and put the lives of American service personnel on the line to maintain a global network of alliances. In the most extreme case, the logic of extended deterrence means that the United States has been prepared to put American cities at risk of nuclear annihilation to defend allies; no commitment could be more consequential. Given these stakes and the other pressing calls on taxpayers, it would hardly be surprising if many Americans wonder whether alliances are still worth it.

The allies don't always help make the case. President Obama was far from the first U.S. leader to complain about allies who don't pull their weight. The burden-sharing debate is as old as the alliances themselves: Western European governments were initially reluctant to assume a share of the defense burden as they struggled to recover after the Second World War, notwithstanding the Soviet threat. The contribution of allies to their own defense and their commitment to collective security often fluctuates, whether as a result of domestic politics, economic pressures, or shifting threat perceptions. For most allies a close security relationship with the United States means they can spend less on their own defense and give priority to domestic priorities—which, absent a major threat, sway more votes than national security.

Many of the United States' oldest and most important alliances are under strain. The implications of Brexit for NATO are not yet clear, but disintegrative forces within Europe and Russian probing in Eastern Europe are already testing alliance solidarity. Relations with Turkey, a vital ally at the crossroads between Europe, the Middle East, and Asia, are fraught following an attempted military coup in July. Frictions with Israel and America's traditional Arab allies in the Middle East over the nuclear deal with Iran have barely been papered over. In the Philippines—geographically key to expanded U.S. military access in Southeast Asia—recently elected President Rodrigo Duterte announced his country's "separation" from the United States and is tilting toward China; defense ties with Thailand, America's other longstanding treaty ally in the region, remain frozen following that country's most recent military takeover. The leadership of South Korea, another vital Asian ally, is roiled by political scandal.

Like the United States, many allies are grappling with weak economic growth, populism, and political gridlock. Preoccupied at home, they are psychologically and materially ill prepared to confront growing threats and challenges abroad—whether Russian adventurism in Eastern Europe and the Middle East, Chinese assertiveness in the Western Pacific, North Korea's march toward a credible intercontinental nuclear strike capability, Iranian designs in the Middle East, or the metastasizing threat posed by ISIL and other Islamist terror networks. The outcome of the recent U.S. election has injected a new element of uncertainty.

It's a bleak picture, and there is little doubt that the United States and the international system in which it has invested so much are at a tipping point because of this toxic brew of external threats and domestic problems. Yet there are good reasons for the United States to keep the faith when it comes to alliances, and to invest in the laborious and time-consuming task of what former Secretary of State George Schultz called "tending the alliance garden."

For one, not all of America's allies are feckless and unreliable. After the 9/11 attacks, NATO and Australia formally invoked their respective security treaties, and both alliances are still fighting in Afghanistan 15 years later. Britain, Germany, and other NATO members are reinforcing their presence in Poland and the vulnerable Baltic states; a number of members are belatedly moving to increase defense spending. Under Prime Minister Shinzo Abe's leadership, not only does Japan meet the vast majority of the cost of supporting U.S. military forces based there but has passed a new security law to allow it to make a greater contribution to international security and has expanded the scope of its alliance responsibilities. Today Australia is enhancing its maritime capabilities and is the second-largest military contributor to the campaign against ISIL in Iraq and Syria. Five other nations are conducting airstrikes against ISIL targets, and a further 25 are making military contributions. South Korea contributed to the multinational intervention force in East Timor in 1999 and deployed 3,500 troops to Iraq in 2003; it recently agreed to host a new U.S. missile-defense system. Alliances build interoperability, relationships, and mutual trust over time that ad hoc coalitions cannot replicate. American allies also make indispensable contributions to global stability through peacekeeping, development assistance, disaster relief, capacity building, and diplomacy.

Just as most allies are lifting their game because they can see that security threats are proliferating, new partners are also stepping forward. In the Middle East, Jordan and the United Arab Emirates are making greater contributions. In Asia, Singapore is hosting U.S. Navy littoral combat ships; a quarter century after the Vietnam war, America has lifted its ban on defense sales, and U.S. Navy ships are once again welcome in Cam Ranh Bay; and defense and security ties with India have been flourishing since the civil nuclear deal reached during the Bush administration. Vulnerable countries in Eastern Europe want closer ties with the United States and the West. In each of these very different regions, countries are reaching out to the United States because they fear the similar threats and share a stake in supporting the international order.

Another good reason not to give up on allies is that there is nothing America's adversaries would like more. In Europe, seeing

NATO dismantled would be top of Vladimir Putin's wish list. Around Asia, Chinese officials chip away with their mantra that long-standing U.S. alliances are a Cold War relic and that America can't be relied on. The Mullahs' vision of a restored Persian empire stretching across the Middle East is only credible if America's alliances with Saudi Arabia, Egypt, and Israel do not hold. Russia, China, and Iran have proxies, catspaws, and temporary partners of convenience; unlike America, however, none has true long-term allies who, for all their faults, are in for the long haul.

The final reason not to give up on America's allies is that there is simply no choice. There are too many threats and challenges for the United States to manage on its own, even if the new Congress repeals the sequester and defense spending is restored and maintained at a higher level. America will need reliable long-term partners who can provide not only military capability but access, intelligence, insights, and a whole range of nonsecurity contributions.

Following an unprecedented presidential election campaign that saw the value of alliances openly questioned, perhaps the bigger question is not whether the United States can rely on its allies but whether they can still rely on the United States. As the incoming Trump administration puts its senior national security team together, its foreign policy direction remains a source of conjecture and uncertainty in Washington and in capitals around the world—particularly those of America's allies. The initial signs are mostly positive: the president-elect has met with the prime minister of Japan, has spoken with many other allied leaders, and has reaffirmed key alliances, including NATO and the major alliances in Asia.

History has shown—and the results of the partial retrenchment of the past eight years have only reinforced—withdrawing from the world and hunkering down will not keep Americans safe. Former Secretary of State Dean Acheson put it best during an earlier period when the United States had to grapple both with rising threats and with national doubts: "We should not pull down the blinds . . . and sit in the parlor with a loaded shotgun, waiting. Isolation was not a realistic course of action. It did not work and it had not been cheap." The siren song of withdrawal that prevailed so disastrously in the 1930s and had to be beaten back in the early 1950s and again in the mid-1970s is being heard once more today. At the start of a new administration, it remains to be seen whether the next generation of U.S. political leaders will rise to the challenge and rally the American people as their predecessors did. One thing is certain: the Republic's allies will be watching closely; so will America's adversaries.

7. HOW MUCH SHOULD WE SPEND ON DEFENSE?

A conversation with Todd Harrison, Andrew Hunter, and Mark Cancian

Craig Cohen and Josiane Gabel: *How is the defense budget environment facing President-elect Trump similar or different from what faced the past two presidents?*

Todd Harrison: President-elect Trump will take office with budget caps already in place that extend through his entire first term. Neither George W. Bush nor Barack Obama entered office with these kinds of statutory constraints on fiscal policy. The budget caps limit the budget options available to the next president and will force him to begin negotiating with Congress right away for some sort of deal that raises the caps.

Another important difference is the deficit and economic outlook. When President Bush took office, the federal government was running a surplus, which made it much easier to increase defense spending while also pursuing other policy priorities like cutting taxes. President Obama took office under an entirely different fiscal situation, with federal deficits soaring due to the recession and the Bush tax cuts. The next president will be entering office under what appears to be a better fiscal situation than eight years ago but a markedly worse fiscal situation than 16 years ago.

Andrew Hunter: The next administration will take office at a very different point in the defense budget cycle than President Obama did. DoD's budget is still bumping along near the bottom after a major budget drawdown. President Obama took office at what we now know was the top of a defense budget cycle, and President Bush took office after a budget drawdown, but one that had been over for two to three years, and with a defense budget that was already rising. The defense budget will almost certainly increase under the next administration, but the question will be how quickly, and how that increase will be used to invest in efficiencies, a cutting-edge workforce, and new capabilities.

Mark Cancian: I'd note that what happens in defense will be a part of what the new administration proposes for the federal budget overall. The current budget agreement does not cover FY 2018, the budget that the administration will need to submit immediately to the Congress, but the caps of the Budget Control Act—which President-elect Trump has said are too low—do continue. So the new administration will need to devise a strategy immediately.

The first budget strategy decision will be whether to work toward some sort of "grand bargain," that is, a deal that includes revenue, entitlements, domestic spending, and defense, and puts the budget on a long-term sustainable path. The Congressional Budget Office's long-term projection shows increasing deficits in the future if nothing is done. Virtually every budget analysis therefore recognizes the need for such a deal, but the politics and budget trade-offs are daunting.

The alternative would be to lift the caps on domestic and defense spending (or one and not the other) and fund them at the higher levels many believe are necessary. Deficit hawks in Congress will oppose such a deal, but it is unclear whether the Freedom Caucus will stand up to a President Trump looking to increase spending on defense.

The fallback is for short-term deals, as has been the case for the last few years. One hopes, however, that a new president and a new Congress can break out of this crisis mode of operation.

Cohen and Gabel: *What are the major budgetary decisions facing the new secretary?*

Cancian: A key decision will be how to implement the president-elect's vision for force expansion. In a September speech, President-elect Trump described his proposal: a regular Army of 540,000 soldiers, a Navy of 350 ships, a Marine Corps of 36 active-duty infantry battalions, and an Air Force of 1,200 active tactical fighter/attack aircraft, plus enhanced missile defense and cyber capabilities. Using CSIS's Force Cost Calculator, we estimate this will cost about $80 billion above what the Obama administration is proposing. On the one hand, that's a lot of money. On the other hand, it would increase the burden on the economy to only about 3.5 percent of GDP, below the level during the wars in Iraq and Afghanistan and far below the level of the Cold War. The challenge will be fitting this expansion into a federal budget proposal that includes other administration priorities like tax cuts and infrastructure rebuilding. The administration will also need to fill in details—which ships, which aircraft, how to recruit the additional personnel. As a complement to building forces, the new leadership in DoD will need to pursue management efficiencies both for potential savings and to convince the public that it is spending this additional money wisely. A recent article in the *Washington Post* claimed that an internal DOD study identified $125 billion in "back office" savings, and that claim engendered much comment about "waste" in DoD. The study did not actually identify any specific savings, instead recommending a process that might find savings, but the point about pursuing efficiencies is important.

Harrison: Another looming budget issue is the "bow wave" of modernization programs, which includes replacement of all three legs of the nuclear triad at roughly the same time. The peak years of funding for major modernization programs occur in the early 2020s. This is just outside the five-year planning horizon now, but it will move into the five-year budget during the next administration. This bow wave in funding for major acquisition programs could be accommodated by increasing the overall DoD budget, cutting other parts of the DoD budget (such as force structure and readiness), cutting smaller acquisition programs, or making trade-offs among major acquisition programs. However, each of these options comes with political and strategic risks. Congress does not appear ready to tackle this complex issue, but the next administration will not be able to avoid making such decisions in its budget requests.

Hunter: The next secretary needs to present the president and Congress with a compelling case for a future years' defense program that meets current global challenges while preparing DoD for the future. This will require significantly more funding that is available under the BCA [Budget Control Act] caps, and so the caps must be negotiated upward. While an overall federal budget solution is a matter outside of the secretary's control, the secretary can and must make the case for what additional defense funding would deliver for our national security now and in the future. The budget dynamics of the last several years have made this nearly impossible, as the political imperative has been to build budgets that maintain maximum negotiating leverage. Because the FY 2018 caps have near zero political support, a window exists for the secretary to lay out this case.

Cohen and Gabel: *How should the new administration handle the Overseas Contingency Operations, or OCO, budget?*

Harrison: Because OCO funding does not count against the BCA budget caps, it has become a convenient tool for Congress and DoD to skirt the budget caps. In the 2017 request, the administration identifies $5.2 billion in OCO funding as being used for base budget activities, but my analysis indicates that an additional $25 billion in funding identified as being for Afghanistan is actually being used for base budget activities. Thus, roughly half of the $59 billion OCO request appears to be used for activities that were previously funded in the base budget. For comparison, base budget funding in OCO under the Bush administration peaked in FY 2008 at $12.1 billion, according to a DoD study.

The problem with using OCO funding to support the base budget, as both Congress and the administration are doing, is that OCO funding does not come with a plan for future years. This means that DoD's current programs and force structure cost more than is shown in its base budget request. If $30 billion in OCO-for-base funding is not made available in the future, deeper cuts in force structure, readiness, and acquisitions will be necessary than what is already projected. A second policy implication is that the higher level of defense spending DoD is assuming in its plans means that overall federal spending and deficit projections will be higher than the administration's FY 2017 budget materials indicate. These additional "enduring" costs would add roughly $120 billion to the $2.6 trillion in deficit spending the budget projects for the next five years (FY 2017 to FY 2021).

It is useful to keep the variable costs of contingency operations separate from the base budget to provide a more accurate picture of what contingency operations cost. For that reason, the next administration should be more disciplined in designating which costs are truly war related and which costs are not. Ideally, all base budget costs would be moved to the base budget and the budget caps would be adjusted accordingly. But if such a deal is not possible, DoD should at a minimum identify in its budget materials how much of the OCO request is actually being used for activities that belong in the base budget and provide a five-year projection for these costs so policymakers can plan accordingly.

Cancian: When war funding began 15 years ago, no one thought it would still be continuing today, but it is and has become a semi-permanent part of the budget landscape. The ideal situation would be a "grand bargain," as discussed earlier. Then the enduring elements of OCO—that is, the elements that would continue after all troops are withdrawn—could be transferred to the base budget. That would align the remaining OCO more closely with the incremental cost of conflicts.

If a grand bargain does not occur, then it's probably not worth expending the political capital trying to move the enduring OCO costs to the base as a stand-alone effort. Democrats in Congress will want commensurate increases in domestic spending. That will be unacceptable to Republicans. Further, as a matter of practical politics, having an OCO "relief valve" that is unconstrained by the budget caps can be helpful in making deals. Instead, the White House might update the criteria that guide what goes into OCO. The criteria could be narrowed to ensure that only the most relevant costs are included in OCO.

Hunter: In a healthy defense budget, the base budget would be large enough to handle known costs and would also include some flexibility for addressing likely contingencies on a small scale. It would also continue to have OCO or something similar to address truly unforeseen contingencies and major unplanned expenses. The current size of the OCO account is driven by the inadequacy of the budget caps. The incoming administration should seek to shift recurring expenses out of OCO to the base budget, but also, to retain OCO at a smaller level as a vital tool in handling an unpredictable world.

Cohen and Gabel: *What future investments should DoD be making now that it has not been able to make?*

Hunter: Three major areas for increased investment come to mind: rapidly evolving enablers, infrastructure, and people. The big modernization programs get all the attention, but often the critical difference comes from the less visible systems such as command, control, and communications and ISR (Intelligence, Surveillance, and Reconnaissance). The next secretary must ensure that the services create the budget space and the buying processes necessary to modernize these enablers at the speed that the underlying technologies are advancing. Investing in science and technology and in essential war-fighting platforms must also remain priorities. DoD needs to get more out of its infrastructure. Given the overall budget situation, there is a strong case for leveraging private capital to invest in a more efficient and capable physical plant. DoD made a major investment in its people by shifting to an all-volunteer force, an investment every bit as important as the high-end technology developments undertaken at the same time that get more attention. Today's budget process doesn't really consider people investments. The military must develop a solid framework for investing in people to ensure continued excellence.

Cancian: As the department has recognized, it will need to increase its investments in advanced capabilities for use against peer-competitors like Russia and China. That's a shift from the focus on counterinsurgency and regional conflicts that the department has had since the end of the Cold War. The Third Offset, which pursues next-generation technologies and concepts to assure military superiority, is intended to develop such capabilities. On the other hand, the department will also need to maintain enough "standard" quality capabilities to fill out its force structure. Not all adversaries will need to be countered with advanced capabilities. That will drive the department to a high/low mix.

Harrison: In recent years, DoD has placed a greater emphasis on protecting and improving the resilience of national security space systems. While funding for space has increased, missile warning and protected satellite communications systems are overdue for follow-on programs. The next administration should make investments in these systems a high priority. It should also increase investments in stealthy unmanned aircraft. The current fleet of unmanned aircraft, such as the MQ-9 Reaper, is consistently in high demand, but the proliferation of advanced air defense systems means that these nonstealthy aircraft may have limited utility in the future. The next generation of unmanned aircraft needs to be stealthy to penetrate defended airspace and built with modularity in mind to carry a wide array of sensors and munitions for strike and surveillance missions.

Cohen and Gabel: Innovation *is the word of the moment. What can the new administration do to work with the private sector to harness the best of U.S. innovation for the defense sector?*

Hunter: The key is presenting the private sector with a business case for investing in innovation that is compelling. Making a range of small bets makes sense. This approach must be accompanied, however, by a system to capitalize on the "wins" that also meaningfully rewards the private sector. But the positive reward of high profits is limited by the relatively small size of the defense market, and the negative incentive of eroding defense market share is complicated by the mutual dependency between DoD and its large suppliers. The best incentive mix is likely to be found in providers of emerging technologies like autonomy and artificial intelligence, where DoD investment can potentially enhance competitiveness outside of the defense market, and where there is less risk to existing supply chains.

Cancian: Looking for additional venues to engage the private sector is helpful, but adding more liaison offices, executive exchanges, and industry conferences has diminishing returns. The key will be getting innovation out of the lab and into operation, and that's where the next administration should focus. As Andrew indicates, it should initiate a lot of small bets that put new capabilities into the field to see how they work. Some will succeed, some will fail, most will need some sort of modification, but there's no substitute for actual experience.

Harrison: Companies tend to mirror their customers. If DoD is not satisfied with the level of innovation it is getting from current defense companies, it should first look in the mirror and try to become a better customer. For example, the current contracting process with DoD is slow, cumbersome, and inefficient. It creates a high barrier to entry for nondefense companies, especially small businesses that cannot afford the overhead it adds to their operations. Being a better customer can help entice more commercial companies to work with the military. But more importantly, it can enable current defense firms to be more innovative, agile, and responsive to the military's needs.

8. DO WE NEED A NEW STRATEGY TO PREVENT TERRORIST ATTACKS ON THE UNITED STATES?

Shannon N. Green

Fifteen years after September 11, terrorism has spread, gained favor among a new generation, and now casts an ever-larger shadow over the globe. The policies of the past two administrations—one Republican and one Democratic—have been successful in hunting down terrorists, destroying their safe havens, and preventing them from planning and executing attacks on the homeland. Despite this good work, the problem has only grown more urgent and severe. New and powerful movements have taken root. Terrorist groups around the world have used technology, the media, religious schools and mosques, and familial and fraternal networks to sell their twisted ideologies, justify their violence, and convince recruits that glory can be found in the mass murder of innocent civilians.

There are no easy solutions to this problem. The United States has taken extraordinary steps to try to address it. These measures include: hardening and expanding physical barriers around sensitive locations and critical infrastructure; improving security procedures and screening at airports and other entry points; tightening controls on people entering the country; and strengthening investigation and prosecution capabilities for terrorism-related cases. More than 263 government entities were either created or reorganized to implement these reforms. Chief among them were the Department of Homeland Security, which integrated all or part of 22 different federal departments and agencies to unify domestic counterterrorism efforts, and the Transportation Security Administration, which centralized and standardized airport security.

The United States simultaneously invested vast sums on countering terrorism abroad and building the capacity of partner security and intelligence services. According to estimates, Congress has appropriated $1.6 trillion to the Department of Defense (DoD) for war-related operational costs since September 11. Intelligence budgets have also significantly increased. In 2007, Congress appropriated $43.5 billion to the National Intelligence Program (NIP). Ten years later, the budget requested for the NIP rose to $53.5 billion. When combined with an estimated $123.2 billion for relevant State Department and Foreign Operations, the executive branch has received almost $2.5 trillion for counterterrorism activities and operations since the 9/11 attacks.

In many respects, the massive human and financial resources devoted to security since September 11 have made us safer. It is more difficult for terrorists to get into the United States and, if they do, harder for them to pull off a complex attack. However, in an era of social media, domestic radicalization, and lone-wolf attacks, it is clear that military, intelligence, and law enforcement strategies alone are insufficient to eradicate the threat. Combating terrorism is both a "battle of arms and a battle of ideas—a fight against the terrorists and their murderous ideology," as the 2006 National Security Strategy put it.

We have undoubtedly failed when it comes to the battle of ideas. Both the Bush and Obama administrations made some attempts to confront extremist ideologies and narratives, but prevention has never received sustained attention and focus, nor has it had the desired effect. One only has to look at the rise of the Islamic State (ISIS) and its unprecedented use of digital platforms to recruit fighters and inspire terrorist attacks all over the world. Instead of continuing to pursue complex 9/11-style attacks, these terrorists have adapted, transitioning to plots that can be executed by small groups or individuals, against soft targets, using less sophisticated and easy-to-acquire weapons. Such attacks do not require extensive training, planning, or coordination, making them harder to spot, but no less lethal. These groups have been better at adapting to our efforts than we have been at adapting to theirs.

Take the way terrorist groups have become more proficient at using social media and modern communications tools to target recruits, build their brand and market share, and expand their reach globally. Personal connections and one-to-one interactions remain central to terrorists' recruitment tactics. But, digital platforms serve as a powerful amplifier and accelerant, allowing terrorist groups to target a much broader audience. Wannabee terrorists can consume propaganda, get inspired, and learn how to execute an attack—without ever leaving their homes. The widespread use of social media has also made violent extremists' plans more difficult to identify and disrupt. Security agencies now have the added challenge of isolating genuine threats from a sea of noise.

Terrorism today is therefore more atomized, pervasive, and challenging to counter than it was at the turn of the century. Going forward, terrorists will likely seek to evade improved law enforcement and intelligence capabilities and border controls by calling on national citizens or green-card holders—without a criminal record or known terrorist ties—to conduct attacks. As such, "homegrown extremism" presents a growing challenge in the United States and elsewhere. Violent extremist groups are also diversifying their recruitment pool, reaching out to women and older and younger generations who are not yet as closely watched by security agencies. Terrorists have already started recruiting children in their preteens—a trend that is likely to accelerate—and women are increasingly found in high-profile roles as supporters, mobilizers, and members of terrorist groups.

This evolution will require a fundamental shift in the way we counter terrorism. We can no longer rely on purely kinetic and law enforcement approaches and expect the same degree of success. Of course, these tools will remain essential for taking terrorists off the battlefield, disrupting plots, and safeguarding our borders. However, if the past 15 years have taught us anything, it is that we will never reduce the violence caused by terrorist groups until we blunt their appeal.

What is needed now is a comprehensive strategy to discredit violent extremists' murderous and twisted ideology and a well-resourced operational plan to confront this threat over the next 15 years. Such a strategy must view terrorism as a global, generational, and ideological struggle. It requires mobilizing and empowering parents, teachers, peers, religious leaders, and other grassroots actors—those closest to would-be terrorists—to detect risks to public safety and intervene quickly to deflect someone from the path of radicalization. Civil society and community leaders are also in the best position to compete with and overtake violent extremists' narratives in virtual and real spaces. However, they need greater political and financial support and training to play this crucial role.

Progress will also require addressing the underlying grievances and aspirations that make individuals open to the siren call of violent extremism. While we know that there is no single variable explaining why people join violent extremist groups, we have learned that terrorism thrives where marginalization, injustice, and oppression reign and where people are struggling to find an authentic identity and sense of purpose. Joining a violent extremist movement is, for many, an aspirational act—an opportunity to gain power, prestige, and status; to address perceived injustice; or to participate in a utopian effort to remake the world.

To prevent catastrophic attacks in the future and protect a new generation from being exploited by terrorist groups, we must find partners willing to help create meaningful opportunities for people to contribute to the political, social, and economic fabric of their societies in positive and sustainable ways. This will require a major reorientation of our approach and surge of investment in bottom-up, civilian-led, and long-term efforts in making communities inhospitable to extremist ideologies and narratives.

9. WHAT ARE THE MAIN RISKS WE FACE IN THE MIDDLE EAST?

Anthony H. Cordesman

The Trump administration faces a wide range of major challenges in the Middle East. Some will have to be dealt with quickly, and others will have to be dealt with over years or decades. Most, however, have two things in common: There is no easy or good U.S. policy option, and no way to avoid serious risks.

Some of these challenges are obvious. They are the logical result of the rise of ISIS and Islamic extremism; legacies from the U.S. invasion of Iraq; threats posed by Iran and the arms race in the Middle East; the new role states like Russia and Turkey are playing in the region; and the range of problems growing out of the fighting in Iraq, Syria, Libya, and Yemen.

During the course of President Trump's first term in office—and beginning almost immediately at the start of his presidency—the United States will need to deal with at least 12 major challenges in the Middle East and North Africa (MENA). The United States must:

- *Rebuild its strategic partnerships with its Arab allies.* The United States retains good military and counterterrorism relations with its Arab allies, but they deeply distrust its level of commitment, relations with Iran, and ability to act decisively and effectively. They also must deal with the fact that a 50 percent cut in petroleum export revenues has sharply altered their ability to modernize their armed forces, and deal with terrorist and extremist movements. One key issue will be whether to provide some form of security guarantees. Another will be to find ways of both reshaping U.S. military capabilities and making allied efforts more effective but less costly.

- *Decide upon the U.S. level of commitment to the defense of the Gulf against Iran, and deal with the full spectrum of Iranian challenges.* These challenges include the uncertainties surrounding Iran's nuclear efforts and the Joint Comprehensive Plan of Action (JCPOA); Iran's expanding its strategic influence in Lebanon, Syria, and Iraq; its search for influence over Shi'ite in the Arab Gulf states and Bahrain; its steady buildup of an asymmetric threat to shipping in and near the Gulf; and the steady growth of its conventionally armed missile and rocket forces.

- *Reshape U.S. counterterrorism efforts to fight the remnants of ISIS—and the full range of other threats from Islamic extremism— in the region.* All of the same forces that generated massive political upheavals in the Arab world in 2011 still exist or have grown much worse. Once (and if) ISIS loses its "caliphate" and ability to control territory in Iraq, Syria, and Libya, the United States and its Arab allies will still face major challenges from Islamic extremists, which interact with deep tribal, sectarian, and ethnic divisions. The United States and Europe will be targets for attacks indefinitely into the future, but the main threat will be in the MENA region and the rest of the Islamic world. The United States must continue to focus on key partnerships with allied Arab states while avoiding actions that will alienate Muslims both in the region and around the world.

- *Find an answer to creating a stable and viable outcome to the Syrian civil war.* Syria is one of the worst challenges the United States faces. Even if some political Band-Aid could be applied, it seems unlikely that any form of ceasefire or division of Syria would prevent Syria from reverting to further conflict unless some broader solution could address its problems with the Assad regime, the Islamic extremist elements in its rebel forces, tensions between Kurds and Arabs, and reducing the role of outside powers. Half of Syria's population is now refugees and internally displaced persons. Stability will prove impossible without providing some hope for these people to return to a normal life. Whatever reality emerges must also bring economic recovery and development to a country that lagged in economic progress and equity for decades before its current political upheavals began in 2011, and which now has only 25 percent or less of the GDP it had in 2011.

- *Help Iraq find some solution to the post-ISIS tensions and divisions between its Sunnis and Shi'ite and Arabs and Kurds.* These efforts cannot be separated from the threat to Iraq posed by an unstable Syria, and the conflicting pressures on Iraq from Iran, Turkey, and outside Arab states. Some form of federalism may be needed, but splitting Iraq into mini-states is an almost certain recipe for further violence and human suffering. Iraq will also need to build security forces capable of deterring Iran, and a nearly bankrupt nation will need to both move toward development and create some form of economic equity to unite its divided regions and factions.

- *Deal with the conflict in Yemen, its steadily rising humanitarian costs, and the challenges in creating lasting security and stability.* Yemen, along with Syria, is one of the most intractable challenges the United States faces. There seems to be little near-term prospect of any form of victory by the Saudi-led, pro-government coalition. The opposing Houthi and Saleh coalition is inherently unstable, and Al Qa'ida in the Arabian Peninsula (AQAP) presents a growing challenge in Sunni areas. Yemen already faced a major structural economic crisis before the civil war began; and food, water, and basic medical care now all present massive human challenges. The choices seem to be nation-building under extraordinarily difficult circumstances or some form of containment that could come only at the cost of immense human suffering.

- *Counter Russia's role in Syria and its expanding influence in the region.* It is unclear that the United States can find any effective way to limit the growth of Russian influence in Syria, or the impact of Russian intervention on regional perceptions of its growing strategic importance. The United States will, however, have opportunities to limit its role as a source of arms and military advisers in other states, and must be ready to deal with major new Russian arms transfers to Iran. The United States can also consider "horizontal escalation" like putting pressure on Russia in other regions such as the Ukraine, just as Russia has done to the United States in Syria. At the same time, the United States must reconsider China's regional role both as another key source of arms sales to Iran, and in creating a new base in Djibouti.

- *Restructure its relations with a post-coup "Erdogan" Turkey whose relations with the United States and Europe have become steadily more authoritarian, and that is intervening actively in Syria and Iraq.* Turkey presents a steadily growing prospect of becoming a repressive and divisive regime that could lock itself into excessive security measures and prolong conflict with its own Kurds while seeking to intervene to deal with Kurds and Turkoman minorities in Syria and Iraq. Turkey will at best be a difficult strategic partner, and is a major "wild card" the Trump administration will have to deal with.

- *Help Egypt achieve security, but influence it to move toward economic recovery and growth, and reduce its current levels of repression and more extreme security measures.* Egypt remains the largest Arab state, and is a key security partner that has provided critical transit rights for U.S. air mobility and through the Suez Canal. The United States will need to help Egypt in its security efforts, and its fight against extremism in the Sinai. It also, however, needs to use its influence to ensure that Egypt addresses its economic strains and places proper limits on its counterterrorism activity and treatment of nongovernmental organizations and legitimate opposition. An open break would only make things worse for both countries, but the United States cannot serve its own interest or Egypt's simply by passively providing security aid.

- *Help other allies like Jordan, Morocco, and Tunisia move toward security and stability.* The United States cannot afford to focus solely on today's problem countries. It needs to help its other regional allies prevent political upheavals, make economic progress and reforms, and establish effective security structures.

- *Fully implement the new security agreements with Israel, but also decide on whether to pursue the two-state solution to the division between Israel and Palestine.* There seem to be few prospects for major progress in peace efforts on either the Israeli or Palestinian side. It is far from clear, however, that the Arab states will remain so preoccupied with other security issues, and Israeli policies and settlements are creating facts on the ground that could make a two-state solution impossible. Simply ignoring the Israeli-Palestinian issue or making largely symbolic efforts may not be enough. The United States must also consider the other aspects of Israel's security: the low-level war in the Sinai, a post-ISIS Syria, and the threat posed by Iranian missiles and links to Hezbollah.

- *Reexamine its calculus as to the strategic importance of the MENA region* in an era where the United States is becoming far less dependent on direct imports of petroleum, but steadily more dependent on the stability and growth of the global economy, and the stable flow of MENA oil and gas exports to Europe and Asia. It is not enough to talk vaguely about vital security interests. The United States needs a full-scale policy analysis to update policies and perceptions based on a very different kind of U.S. dependence on the secure flow of Gulf petroleum exports.

This list of challenges would be daunting at any time, but the United States also faces major domestic needs as well as other foreign challenges in dealing with Russia and Europe, the war in Afghanistan, and the emergence of China and security issues in Asia. It also is all too clear from the recent past that the United States cannot predict whether and when new challenges will rise in any of these regions.

Equally important, there are no "good" or simple options open to the United States in any of these 12 cases. Each case is driven by forces that mean it will probably still exist in some form after the president's first term. Some cases already have persisted in some form for decades.

Like it or not, the Trump administration is inheriting a list of complex problems that it has to address simultaneously, all of which involve "long games" that have significant risks. There is no place in the MENA region for either passivity or the traditional description of the U.S. rush to action: finding solutions that are simple, quick, and wrong.

10. WHAT OPTIONS DO WE HAVE IN SYRIA?

Melissa G. Dalton

As President-elect Trump assumes office in January, Syria will be among the most urgent foreign policy challenges he and his new team will have to tackle. Syria's civil war has raged for five years, beginning as peaceful protests against the brutality of President Bashar al-Assad's regime and descending into a deadly spiral, with over five hundred thousand killed, millions of refugees and internally displaced persons (IDPs), and thousands besieged by regime and Russian attacks. The United States and the international community have struggled to effectively address the crisis in Syria. There truly are no good policy options at this point, as all choices entail significant risks. The U.S. public wants a strong America but does not want to become embroiled in another conflict on the scale of the post–9/11 interventions in Iraq and Afghanistan. However, the current limited approach in Syria has been quite costly to U.S., allied, and partner interests and arguably has diminished U.S. leadership credibility across the globe. A Trump administration will have the opportunity to change the course of U.S. Syria policy. This essay, based in part on a scenario-based workshop CSIS hosted in November 2016 on Syria, lays out the range of options on the table on Day One.

CURRENT STATE-OF-PLAY

The grinding Syrian civil war has grown increasingly intense and sectarian over the past three years. It has pit Syrian government forces and their foreign allies, including Russia and Iran, against a range of antigovernment insurgents. These opposition fighters include the Islamic State (ISIS) and al-Qaida affiliate Jubhat Fateh al-Sham (JFS, formerly Jubhat al-Nusra), as well as a constellation of Syrian Kurdish and Arab rebels, who are supported by the United States, other Arab countries, and Turkey. U.S. and coalition strikes on ISIS and JFS have reduced their numbers to approximately 17,000 and 7,000, respectively, in the region comprising Syria and Iraq. The United States reportedly has 300 special operations forces in Syria and has conducted over 1,900 air strikes since May 2016 with anti-ISIS coalition members.

Russia currently has 4,000 troops in Syria. Its intervention in 2015 has since enabled the Syrian government to reinforce its positions, retake some territory from Syrian rebels, and regain Aleppo, using brutal tactics against Syrian civilians and civilian targets including the targeting of hospitals and schools. Assad's Syrian Armed Forces currently fields somewhere in the neighborhood of 300,000 troops. Further buttressing Assad's forces, Iran has mobilized up to 115,000 fighters in Syria, comprised of Lebanese Hezbollah, Syrian, Iraqi, Afghan, and Pakistani recruits. Taken together, there is a significant fighting force with active supply lines from external allies backing Assad.

The Syrian Democratic Forces and other Syrian groups supported by the United States and its coalition partners number approximately 40,000 to 50,000 soldiers. They successfully pushed ISIS out of areas in northern Syria in 2016. Substantial governance and security challenges, however, remain in the recovered areas. For one, Turkey's intervention in northern Syria has complicated U.S. and partnered security efforts, as U.S. and Turkish objectives clash with regard to the role and reach of Syrian Kurdish forces. Additionally, Arab-Kurd tensions present a specter of a civil war to come.

U.S. INTERESTS AND OBJECTIVES IN SYRIA

Historically, Syria itself has not held great strategic importance for the United States, even though it has long been viewed in the region as a geographic prize located between the two great river systems of the Nile and Euphrates. Syria today stands at the epicenter of a regional conflict with global consequences for U.S. interests and objectives. This is a multifaceted conflict destabilizing the region and Europe and raising the possibility of a broader war. Achieving U.S. objectives in Syria may require inherent tradeoffs in the policy choices the new U.S. administration might pursue. These interests and objectives could include: countering terrorism (not just terrorists, but also the roots of terrorism); strengthening relations with regional allies and partners, with particular emphasis on Turkey; preventing military confrontation with Russia and Iran, while limiting the long-term, subversive influence they might have in Syria; demonstrating cohesion and effectiveness of U.S. allies and partners; preventing conflict from further destabilizing neighboring states and Europe; limiting human suffering; and working toward the eventual goal of improved governance in Syria. It is likely that only some of these goals could be achieved, and possibly at the expense of others. Inherent in resolving the tensions among these interests will be determining the priority afforded to Syria as an issue to tackle within the Trump administration and how they see its importance relative to other global interests.

POSSIBLE POLICY CHOICES

The next administration will choose a Syria policy from a range of known options, most of which are not mutually exclusive and several of which have been attempted at least in part by the Obama administration. All options in Syria entail risks and trade-offs— including choices of inaction or tacit acceptance of the status quo. This requires the Trump administration to determine what is most important to U.S. short- and long-term interests. The four basic choices are as follows:

I. *Allow Russia and Iran to back Assad in consolidating the Aleppo-to-Damascus corridor.* This could be an intentional policy choice or simply the outcome of events on the ground continuing on their current course. If the new administration drags its heels on making a decision on Syria, this may well be the result regardless of intent. Assad and Russia have nearly secured Aleppo and will likely press on to Idlib next, where JFS and other opposition groups have embedded among civilians. Under this option, the United States could abandon its insistence that Assad must go and make a deal with the Russians to ensure continued counterterrorism efforts against ISIS and JFS. Washington could also reduce support to local Syrian rebels in order to de-escalate tensions with Russia, Assad, and Turkey. The United States could still maintain support for international humanitarian operations in Syria, the neighboring region, and in Europe, but Washington would cease to try to curb Assad's or Russian targeting of civilian populations.

The risks to this approach begin inside Syria. A deep-seated Sunni insurgency would likely continue to challenge Assad throughout much of the country, providing fertile ground for terrorist recruitment and providing safe haven for terrorist groups. Even if the United States stands down on its efforts to train and equip resistance groups, regional partners may still support local Syrian groups to combat Assad and Iranian influence. Refugee and IDP flows will worsen with Assad's consolidation, putting additional pressure on Lebanon, Jordan, Turkey, Iraq, and Europe. A Russian- and Iranian-protected Assad enclave in the Middle East, ringed by Iranian-backed militias, could serve as a beachhead for attacks against Israel, Turkey, and other allies, or even U.S. interests at points in the not-so-distant future. It is also unclear whether Russia would be satisfied with this foothold in the Middle East or if it would harbor grander ambitions to reclaim all of Syria or even to look beyond its borders. Beyond Syria, U.S. strategic and moral credibility and resolve would be questioned if we were to walk away from a long-standing policy to contest Assad, even if it were to come with a change of administration. Certainly America's moral suasion would suffer.

2. *Strengthen the counterterrorism approach to defeat ISIS and al-Qaida.* The president-elect made it clear in his campaign that he wants to more robustly counter ISIS. A strengthened counterterrorism approach would likely include targeting JFS, enhancing intelligence collection, reinforcing U.S. and regional strategic forces presence and force enablers in Syria, and increasing air strikes on ISIS and JFS targets. A counterterrorism policy "on steroids" could also tie together the campaigns against ISIS in Raqqa, Syria, and in Mosul, Iraq, to more effectively squeeze ISIS with greater operational synchronization. The United States might choose to cooperate with Russia and Assad (and thus also Iran) to degrade ISIS and JFS, as these countries might provide ground forces and intelligence.

This approach may reduce immediate terrorist threats and accomplish a major policy goal of the incoming administration. The potential downside is that it does not address underlying challenges or grievances that are rooted in the political, economic, identity, and social dynamics that produce terrorists. In other words, for every terrorist we capture or kill, three could take their place, particularly if there is no attempt to hold territory or invest in a political solution or improved governance. Such a policy would undoubtedly worsen humanitarian conditions, as Assad would be able to indiscriminately target civilians with impunity under the guise of countering terrorism. The United States would be seen as complicit in these activities and as a partner to Assad, Russia, and Iran, further inflaming longer-term Sunni terrorist movements against the West. As such, it would risk significant blowback from regional Arab partners on other priorities such as Israeli and Gulf security and efforts to pressure Iran into normalizing and moving away from its pursuit of nuclear weapons. This approach also fails to contain spillover effects, including the possibility that the conflict moves across borders, extremist group exfiltration, and refugee flows into neighboring countries and Europe.

3. *Conduct a larger-scale military intervention to pressure Assad.* This choice involves the greatest departure from the status quo and would require heavy resourcing and commitment and likely a vote of affirmation from Congress. A U.S. intervention could take the form of implementing no-fly zones, safe zones, enhanced support for Syrian rebels, and/ or coercive measures and direct strikes on Assad regime targets. Almost all of these types of interventions require a larger ground force commitment to enforce a change in the military balance, pressure Assad, and create a safe area for humanitarian response efforts. On the high end of ground force requirements under these options, up to 30,000 ground forces could be required to secure a safe zone. This number would include local Syrian, regional, and U.S. and Coalition troops.

The major downside to pursuing this option is that it heightens the potential for miscalculation or escalation with Russia and Iran. Turkey is also likely to resist an intervention if the United States relies upon Syrian Kurdish forces to secure areas, which we undoubtedly would. Syrian rebels with ISIS or JFS sympathies could infiltrate safe zones and conduct attacks or gather intelligence for ISIS and JFS. As Afghanistan and Iraq have demonstrated, large concentrations of U.S. troops can never be perfectly secured. U.S. and coalition ground troops would be magnets for terrorist attacks and a beacon for terrorist recruitment. Such a policy would involve high up-front risks to U.S. and international security and resourcing costs but could accrue gains in local Syrian governance and security over time if part of a greater political strategy for Syria and the region. If the military requirements of the intervention are such that the involvement of U.S. ground troops becomes necessary—a likely reality—then the near-term risk to American lives and treasure could be great.

4. *Pursue a negotiated political outcome to remove Assad.* The president-elect and his advisers have expressed openness to dealing with Russia but appear to want a hardline tack versus Iran. On Syria, it will be difficult to pursue both goals. Iran will need to be on board with any diplomatic deal involving Syria if such a deal is to endure. It is unlikely that the Russians hold enough leverage over Iran to compel cooperation or that Iran will necessarily see the removal of Assad as in its interests. Washington will likely need to adopt a range of approaches, including carrots and sticks, to persuade Russia and Iran to come to the table. It is unclear exactly what the right mix will be, but it likely will require a more extensive coalition of allies and partners. For example, the United States and Europe could provide sanctions relief to Russia in exchange for Russia pressuring Assad to leave. This could include overt and covert pressure on Assad himself and his inner circle, including enhancing financial pressure, information and cyber operations, or possibly limited air strikes on Syrian air bases to ground Syrian air attacks. There is certainly no guarantee that the Russians would accept such a course or in accepting would abide by their commitments. Further concessions to Russia might include permitting a sustained Russian military presence in Syria and in the Eastern Mediterranean. Iran will want a pliable replacement to Assad to preserve its influence and access, including Hezbollah's supply and operational reach in the Levant. It's no guarantee that Assad's replacement under such conditions would necessarily yield better results vis-à-vis U.S. interests. The phasing of the negotiations might include starting with creating "no bomb zones," and instituting a true cessation of hostilities. Negotiations could eventually include Syrian opposition leaders, so that

Syrians own the solution and the negotiated outcome is
more likely to endure.

This is by far the hardest outcome to achieve, as it must
have both multilateral and local buy-in for it to endure, and
parties to the conflict have competing agendas and interests.
It is likely the only option that will de-escalate the overall
violence in Syria quickly, but very well could require
escalation against Russia, Assad, and Iran to achieve it.
This is perhaps a U.S. form of the Russian doctrine of
"escalate to de-escalate," and will require a very nuanced
approach to avoid miscalculation. Moreover, absent a shift
in the local balance of power, the United States would enter
such negotiations with limited leverage, as Secretary
Kerry's negotiations with the Russians have already shown.
Perhaps the Trump administration can generate its own
leverage, but even if successful, the new administration
would be seen as complicit in the actions of Russia, Iran, and
the Assad regime against the Syrian people, a high cost to
pay to U.S. credibility.

FUNDAMENTAL STEPS TO CHANGE THE COURSE

Regardless of the Trump administration's policy preferences on Day
One, it would be wise to consider the following six elements in its
approach to Syria. First, it should align covert and noncovert approaches into a coherent strategy. Second, it should find ways to
increase U.S. leverage against Russia and Iran, including through
coercive actions. Third, it should strengthen planning and coordination against ISIS targets across Syria and Iraq, including synchro-
nizing operations for Raqqa and Mosul. Fourth, it should work
with regional allies and partners to craft a coordinated political
and military approach for dealing with Assad and countering terrorism and its underpinnings. Fifth, even if it seeks to accommodate
Russia, Iran, and Assad, it should work with the international
community to provide emergency humanitarian assistance to
besieged areas, with clear and immediate repercussions in the

case of outside interference. Sixth, the United States and whomever it chooses to work with in Syria should set the conditions now for what comes after ISIS and JFS, amplifying support to, and knitting connections among, local Syrian security forces and governance structures. The complexity and severity of the Syria challenge demands tough choices and committed U.S. leadership. Come January, the next administration has an opportunity to chart a better pathway forward.

11. WHAT ARE THE KEY ENERGY CHOICES FOR THE NEW ADMINISTRATION?

Sarah O. Ladislaw

The United States is blessed with ample natural resources, a strong economy, a vibrant system of universities and civil society groups, and world-class private companies. Each has contributed to the United States' position as one of the largest energy producers and consumers in the world, and a leading source of innovative energy technologies.

The United States faces a world in which the energy system is very much in a state of flux. Oil markets are slowly coming back into balance after two years of oversupply accompanied by a dramatic fall in prices. The future price trajectory is uncertain—even with OPEC's recent decision to cut output. A bumpy ride at lower price levels seems likely, and one cannot discount the possibility of major price spikes driven by supply disruption.

Economic headwinds and uncertainty in major economies like China are likely to weigh on expectations for energy demand growth in all parts of the world. Technological, policy, and market changes continue to reshape established and developing electric power sectors in terms of generation mix, efficiency, and complexity of the grid. Geopolitical turmoil in certain key energy-producing regions of the world will continue to keep oil and gas markets on edge. A wave of populism, antiglobalization, and political discontent continues to weaken institutions and create a crisis of governance in many countries around the world.

On the climate front, the United States has established itself as a leader of global climate action and emissions reduction—but a huge amount of additional progress is needed to meet the stated global targets. Meanwhile, the center of gravity of global energy demand growth has shifted to developing countries, making those regions the landscape of the bulk of new energy investment and leading all energy sector stakeholders to focus on connecting the world's poorest to modern energy services.

The election of Donald Trump as president has been characterized as an abrupt right turn for U.S. energy and climate change policies. Trump's campaign promises include rolling back environmental regulations, opening up more areas of oil and gas development, revitalizing the coal industry, pulling out of the Paris Climate Agreement, and making the U.S. energy independent. In reality the Trump administration can take action toward each of these objectives, but their impact will be somewhat constrained by process and market forces.

For example, the process to roll back Obama-era leasing policies and environmental regulations is onerous and litigious, yielding very little long-term certainty for investors in the affected sectors. Climate change is the area most affected by these changes, despite the aforementioned uncertainty. Federal climate-related policies that would have expanded under a Clinton administration will almost certainly not advance (there is speculation over whether the state and local-level complements to those policies may continue to hold). In the context of the global climate agenda that was seeking even greater emissions reductions than pledged in Paris, simply holding the line on U.S. emissions reduction achieved to date is suboptimal, taking actions that increases emissions could be disastrous.

Another example is the pledge to deliver energy independence, a goal the United States is closer to achieving today than any time in the last 40 years. Today, the United States is producing more energy than ever relative to its consumption and yet, it is just as tied to the fate of other countries as it was a decade ago, when our reliance on imported energy was at its highest. It is unclear whether or not any of Donald Trump's vague statements about standing up to OPEC and advancing energy independence will materialize as anything other than pro-energy production policies which will be welcomed by the oil, gas, and coal industry, but investments may be limited by an oversupplied global market, at least in the next couple of years, and actual production impacts may be limited by the longtime cycles involved in new investments coming to fruition. As for the U.S. posture toward OPEC and other major oil producers and consumers, this will likely be more affected by other foreign policy issues, like our stance on trade, changes to the Iran nuclear agreement, and other security issues.

As with other new administrations, Trump will inherit an energy system with its own dynamics and issues—only part of which is under federal control. These days the energy sector is undergoing some profound changes that will provide both obstacles and opportunities for the new administration to shape our collective energy future.

Take, for example, the U.S. electric power sector. Just eight short years ago, half of U.S. power generation was met by coal; that is down to 32 percent due to abundant natural gas resources, stricter environmental standards on coal-fired power plants, and an increase in solar and wind capacity. The trend away from coal is likely to continue absent very significant government support. The U.S. has abundant gas resources, and existing state and federal policies and tax incentives, along with the declining cost of renewables, will keep renewables competitive. States across the country are experimenting with new pricing and regulatory models to accommodate a host of distributed energy resources from rooftop solar, to energy storage and demand response technologies. All the while electricity demand in the United States is flat to declining because of lower economic growth and higher efficiency rates, meaning that large changes to the fuel mix push out other sources. These trends will continue to challenge the role of coal and nuclear power.

Eight nuclear reactors have announced plans to close, and by some estimates, 15 to 20 more are likely to follow suit. Early next year the U.S. District Court will decide the fate of the first-ever sector-wide standard for carbon dioxide regulation as part of the Clean Power Plan regulation. The Trump administration has pledged to roll back this regulation along with many other environmental regulations affecting the U.S. electric power sector. While the new administration has the authority to undertake certain deregulation, the process will be long, and the government will be sued by states and environmental organizations. The outcome will be greater uncertainty rather than a clear signal toward more or less climate regulation over the lifetime of the long-term investments. Stakeholders across the sector recognize that these changes are stressing a system whose physical and regulatory structure was designed for a different time, and changes must take place to accommodate the new realities of a system in transition.

Change is taking place in the transportation sector as well. The U.S. vehicle fleet has caught up with its international competitors in terms of fleet efficiency for the first time in decades. Ride and vehicle sharing is a growing phenomenon in most urban centers, and the technology that enables it is largely considered to be the precursor for an entirely new transportation experience brought about by the eventual advent of fully autonomous vehicles. Amidst all this change the nation's transportation system is stuck in a time warp. Highways, bridges, and rail systems remain woefully under-maintained and pose safety hazards as well as a general drag on the economy. Many state and local communities are modernizing their transit infrastructure, but much more can and should be done. The Trump administration campaigned on a promise to invest in the nation's infrastructure, much of which includes the transportation sector. Smart infrastructure policies and reinvestments could be a very welcome and needed advancement in this sector.

Meanwhile, the U.S. oil and gas production revolution continues. Despite two years of low oil and natural gas prices, U.S. production remains higher than it has been in decades. U.S. oil production is playing a central role in global oil market dynamics, and U.S. natural gas exports are being used as a symbol of the potential for a larger role for gas in the coming decades. Concerns over the environmental impact of production, especially onshore, has spawned efforts by advocacy groups to stop producing all fossil fuels by directly targeting pipeline infrastructure development projects to ensure large onshore resources do not get developed. Ironically this is happening at the same time that much of the nation's oil and gas infrastructure is reaching maturity and is in need of replacement. Several recent oil spills and gas leaks speak to the need to update and maintain this infrastructure. Building new pipelines like Keystone XL and Dakota Access will get the most political attention in a new administration, but the challenge to modernize existing pipeline infrastructure and continuing to improve the environmental performance of the nation's burgeoning oil and gas production will be critically important to address as well.

The new administration has a tremendous opportunity to harness these changes and make some much-needed reinvestments that will benefit the U.S. economy, and can even choose to do so in a way that is acceptable to both political parties. One of the few areas of agreement in this year's deeply divided race for the presidency was the need to rebuild the nation's infrastructure and use the energy sector as a source for job creation and growth. While one party favored growth from so-called clean energy sources and the other focused more on oil, natural gas, and coal, the underlying recognition of potential opportunity was present in both political parties. Several bills drafted in the current Congress, as well as the U.S. Department of Energy through its *Quadrennial Energy Review* and the U.S. Department of Transportation with its *Beyond Traffic* report, have laid out some good ideas about current infrastructure needs and challenges that must be addressed to face the energy infrastructure challenges of the future. The Trump administration would do well to rely on these documents and the insights they provide to inform its decisionmaking.

Another area of bipartisan agreement is on the innovation agenda. The United States is a world leader in energy, automotive, and agricultural technologies of all varieties and supporting the innovation ecosystems that allow that competitive advantage to thrive is another area where real contributions to our long-term energy outlook can be achieved.

One final key message from this year's election experience is that there is a great deal of dissatisfaction in both parties about the status of economic and social mobility. This concern is likely to permeate energy debates at the national and local level on both the right and the left of the political spectrum because energy is often tied to economic opportunity and job creation. For the last several elections both political parties have suggested that economic growth at both a national and local level could be achieved either through low-carbon energy deployment or fossil-based energy production and low energy prices. What no politician is willing to admit is that our understanding of how energy fits into economic and social mobility is underdeveloped and self-serving. This is an area where a bipartisan effort to truly understand energy's role in social and economic mobility and improve our policies and investments would make a lot of sense.

Energy plays an important strategic role in the strength of the U.S. economy and our relationships with other countries. While the Trump administration's campaign agenda will be constrained by both process and market factors, a dynamic energy industry affords a great many opportunities as well. They are opportunities worth taking.

12. WHAT COULD A U.S.-MEXICO PARTNERSHIP LOOK LIKE?

Kimberly Breier

When the Trump administration takes office in January 2017, one of the clearest articulations of its foreign policy is likely to be its position toward a range of issues at the center of U.S-Mexico relations. Three of the centerpieces of the Trump campaign involved issues closely tied to the bilateral relationship: the need to improve border security, reform the immigration system, and address job creation and trade in a globalized world. If handled properly, new approaches could advance cooperation with Mexico, not threaten it, as is assumed by many Mexico watchers. Handled badly, though, the downside risks are serious for U.S. interests. A major bilateral rift could ripple into Mexican internal politics in unpredictable ways, for both Mexico and the United States, as well as threaten U.S. economic security and competiveness in global markets.

UNDERSTANDING MEXICO'S CURRENT CHALLENGES

As the Trump administration begins to identify its first priorities, Mexico will be entering into a presidential election cycle for its summer 2018 contest, which will add complexity to government-to-government talks. Only about 25 percent of Mexicans approve of the job being done by President Enrique Peña Nieto, an unprecedented low for a government with two years left in office. The public is highly dissatisfied with government, fueled in part by the economic downturn, high-profile cases of corruption and impunity, and persistent insecurity.

Mexico's economic growth has been in steady decline in recent years. The United States is Mexico's largest export market, and demand in the U.S. market has slowed since the 2008 financial crisis. Low oil prices also have had a negative effect on the Mexican economy given its role as an energy supplier and on the federal budget as close to a third of the public monies derive from oil revenues. Corruption continues to erode public confidence in the Mexican political system, as it has in other countries throughout Latin America in recent years. It has also roused a private sector that feels squeezed between increased taxation pressure and the costs of corruption. Cartel-fueled violence and petty street crime continues throughout the country, as promises by the Peña Nieto government to reduce violence levels have not yet been fulfilled.

MEXICO'S OVERALL TRAJECTORY OF REFORM

It is important to recognize, however, that the current challenges facing Mexico do not occur in a vacuum, and Mexico's overall trajectory is one of dramatic reform of the state. It would be hard to find a nation-state elsewhere in the world that has undergone a political and economic modernization as fast and deep as Mexico, particularly over the past two decades.

On the political front, Mexico struggled during the twentieth century to emerge as a multiparty democracy. The political system that emerged from the Mexican Revolution in 1910–1920 was dominated by the Institutional Revolutionary Party (PRI), which held presidential power continually for 71 years. Its hegemony began to loosen when the left-of-center Revolutionary Democratic Party (PRD) won control of Mexico City (Cuauhtémoc Cárdenas) in 1997—a post that the PRD has held continually since. Then, the presidential election victory of the National Action Party (PAN) in 2000 (Vicente Fox) and 2006 (Felipe Calderón) and then the return to PRI-rule in 2012 (Peña Nieto) defied those who argued that a peaceful transfer of power from one party to another in Mexico was beyond reach. There have been other encouraging signs as well. Mexico's Congress is no longer the rubber stamp it once was. And, in 2012, Mexico's main political parties passed a reform platform under the "Pact for Mexico" focused on much-needed internal reforms including in the areas of education, labor, the electoral system, fiscal policy, telecommunications, and the historic opening of the energy sector to private investment. Overall, Mexico is a more democratic country now than it was 20 years ago, although with all of the fits and starts that comes with it.

Mexico's economy has also been dramatically transformed over this same period. Prior to the 1990s, Mexico's economy was largely closed to imports, including from the United States. The North American Free Trade Agreement (NAFTA) played a transformative and positive role in opening up the Mexican economy, creating jobs, and in the expansion of Mexico's middle class. Mexico now has 10 free trade agreements involving 45 countries and a host of other investment deals involving another 33. On economic policy in recent years, Mexico has moved to increase competition in telecommunications as well as undertaking the historic opening of the energy sector to private investment following the nationalization of the 1930s.

STALLED PROGRESS AND A CRITICAL WINDOW OF OPPORTUNITY

Despite the fast-forward transformation of the economy and political system, the reform process for law enforcement and the judiciary is often described by Mexican analysts, foreign investors, and, more importantly, by public opinion as more disappointing. Despite numerous restructurings of law enforcement, insecurity prevails in many parts of the country. The landmark judicial reform passed in 2008 that is transforming the judiciary from a closed inquisitorial system toward an adversarial model is yet to be fully implemented. The slow progress on rule-of-law issues has created enormous opportunity costs for Mexico in terms of trade and investment, and public confidence in institutions remains low.

The next two years in Mexico are a critically important window for reform implementation. Moreover, the population's *perception* of the success of implementation may be even more important than formal passage of reform bills into law. Justice reform implementation amid continuing impunity for the political class will not be perceived as a real change. Energy and telecommunications reforms that do not deliver benefits to average Mexicans are not likely to be seen as transformative, even though the rules on paper are a dramatic departure from the *status quo ante.* A failure by the Mexican government to fundamentally shift the momentum against the cartels and against corrupt practices in the public sector will further erode confidence in institutions and governance. The opportunity to strengthen the Mexican state and consolidate the reforms rests in the hands of the Mexican political class.

Much of Latin America has seen the winds of political change blowing through the region in the past two years. For Mexico, it may well be that public perception of the political class and its actions in the next two years will influence how strong the winds of change blow in Mexico in 2018. This is of critical importance to the United States, because political uncertainty on the southern U.S. border could impact bilateral cooperation across the range of issues in the relationship.

THE U.S.-MEXICO RELATIONSHIP

As one of only two land neighbors, Mexico is a critical partner of the United States on both national security and economic security. Despite this fact, U.S. policy toward Mexico often lacks a "big-think" vision that recognizes both the breadth and depth of issues that matter greatly to the American people. The relationship often gets out of balance and ends up in a reactive, tit-for-tat cycle. This is deeply counterproductive and must be avoided if for no other reason than to ensure that the two governments deliver results.

The priorities outlined by President-elect Trump during the campaign, including immigration reform and border security improvements, suggest a quick focus on Mexico. Done carefully, an immigration reform can be a win-win, and border security upgrades would include not only more physical barriers, but stepped-up cooperation and a focus on border infrastructure. Any border security measures must take into account that US$2.4 billion worth of goods cross the United States' northern and southern borders *every day*. The goal should be to balance security challenges with the needs of cross-border commerce that are fundamental to the U.S. economy.

In fact, the Trump administration has a great opportunity to put serious attention on border infrastructure, which is a long-neglected issue and a drag on U.S. competitiveness. Mexican and Canadian leaders have also made infrastructure a priority, and cooperation in this area could present an early win all around. The three countries need to work together to prioritize what new points of entry are needed and also on how to fund new projects. Recent estimates suggest that border infrastructure improvements in North America could increase U.S. GDP by one percentage point, or about US$220 billion a year, creating new jobs along with it.

The Trump campaign emphasized the need for the United States to get better deals on trade. If it pursues trade discussions, they must be framed by the reality that the U.S. economic relationship with Mexico is not a zero-sum game. U.S. companies and the products they produce are competitive in the global economy in part thanks to imported components from Mexico and Canada. In fact, the private sectors in the United States and Mexico and Canada not only trade with each other, but make products together with supply chains that are deeply integrated. Those ties have made the United States more competitive in the global marketplace, and far from being a net liability, are an asset.

The starting point of any discussions should also recognize that NAFTA dramatically increased U.S. exports to Mexico. In 1992, prior to NAFTA, U.S. exports to Mexico totaled about US$42 billion. In 2015, the United States exported goods and services valued at US$267 billion, making it the United States' second-largest export market and the source of millions of U.S. jobs. The total two-way trade in goods and services in 2015 was over US$580 billion.

While it is not clear what the priorities the administration would have in a NAFTA discussion (Mexico gave up more on tariffs than did the United States in 1993), it is important to recognize that all parties agree that NAFTA could be looked at with modern eyes and that there is an opportunity to do this in a win-win-win fashion. In fact, the three countries already began to modernize the deal, under the talks for the now-stalled Trans Pacific Partnership (TPP). TPP talks included Canada and Mexico, and all sides agreed to add new labor and environment provisions, as well as subjecting them to dispute settlement mechanisms. Additional low-hanging fruit of a NAFTA discussion could include issues as mundane as visa categories—occupations that exist now in the technology sector, for example, did not exist 22 years ago. When NAFTA was conceived, the Internet did not exist. New rules are needed for sectors like e-commerce. Mexico's energy sector was not open to private investment when NAFTA was negotiated. The three countries now have the opportunity to work together toward North American energy independence with all of the positive geostrategic implications that could have.

Done properly, both the United States and Mexico (and Canada) could find benefits from the process of updating the trade relationship and addressing issues including the skills gap across the continent, particularly in manufacturing. For those who have lost jobs due to globalization, the three countries could revisit adjustment assistance and job-training programs to help our three societies better adapt and ensure that skills match jobs already available. According to recent estimates, the number of manufacturing jobs unfilled in the United States because of a skills gap numbers in the millions. North America has the opportunity to tackle these issues as allies, not competitors.

Further, Mexico's prosperity is in the interest of the United States. A stronger Mexican economy means fewer Mexicans will leave their homes seeking opportunity in the United States. (Net immigration flows from Mexico are already less than zero, according to a 2015 Pew study.) Strong growth and job creation in Mexico also spur the expansion of Mexico's middle class and make Mexico a better partner as citizens' demands, for improved security and rule of law, for example, dovetail with U.S. security interests.

Outside of the economic relationship, the United States has a direct stake in Mexico's success in strengthening its security and rule of law. The U.S. Mérida Initiative was conceived to support implementation of Mexico's rule-of-law reforms, recognizing the fundamental importance of working with Mexico to address organized crime, violence, and impunity and its effects in both countries. There is much more that could be done to weaken the influence of the cartels responsible for exporting drugs into the United States, but success will depend primarily on U.S.-Mexican intelligence and law enforcement partnerships and the mutual sharing of information. That is, success in this area will center around trust and would be at risk in a climate of confrontation.

Both Mexico and the U.S.-Mexico relationship stand at a crossroads. With thought and care, the relationship could enhance both countries' security and prosperity in the years ahead. Handled badly, the outcome would be mutually destructive. The stakeholders in the U.S.-Mexico relationship include not only the federal governments, but the private sectors, state and local governments, millions of workers whose jobs depend on trade, and millions of citizens who are involved in daily interactions with their families or business partners across the border. It is critically important for both sides to get this right, as the downside risks are too great not to.

13. HOW CAN MULTILATERAL INSTITUTIONS WORK IN AMERICA'S INTEREST?

Daniel F. Runde and Conor M. Savoy

Seventy years ago, at the Bretton Woods conference, the United States was instrumental in creating a system of multilateral financial institutions that came to be known as the "Bretton Woods institutions." Initially consisting of the World Bank Group, the International Monetary Fund (IMF), and what became the World Trade Organization, these entities sought to rebuild the global economic order destroyed by the Great Depression and World War II. Beginning in the 1950s, as European colonies gained their independence, the World Bank shifted from rebuilding Europe to focus more on supporting economic development in sub-Saharan Africa and developing Asia. Decolonization and the Cold War competition with the Soviet Union also triggered the formation of a series of regional development banks (African Development Bank, Asian Development Bank [ADB], and the Inter-American Development Bank) that provide more specialized lending and technical assistance. At the end of the Cold War, a regional bank focused on the former Soviet republics and Central Eastern Europe was set up, the European Bank for Reconstruction and Development. These were created firmly in a Cold War (or post–Cold War) context and required U.S. and allied leadership to establish. This system remains a significant source of development finance today.

The multilateral development banks (MDBs) face an uncertain future. There are new sources of development finance, new multilateral institutions challenging the established norms, and new areas of focus. To be sure, though, the MDBs continue to demonstrate their value. In the wake of the 2008–2009 global financial crises, the MDBs and IMF stepped in to provide significant financial support in developing and emerging market countries. This was needed as commercial banks and lenders stepped back from lending to manage their balance sheets. The United States remains the largest or second-largest shareholder in all of these institutions; this reflects the historical role it played in founding them, but it also reflects the fact that the United States made and makes significant financial contributions to support their operations. The United States must take the lead in overhauling the MDBs to make them more effective to meet the challenges of the next 15 years.

The consequences of the United States failing to act are not academic and quite clear to see. The Trump administration and Congress need to recognize that delay or indecision about the MDBs will have negative consequences to U.S. influence and prestige by creating opportunities for competitors such as China to step into the void. With the seeming rejection of the Trans-Pacific Partnership by the incoming administration and others, China recently announced that it would revive its own regional free-trade pact that would likely exclude the United States. This, coupled with the recently launched Asian Infrastructure Investment Bank (AIIB), means that China is moving ever closer to cementing an alternative system—that follows different standards and rules—to the U.S.-led system of the past 70 years. This is something that the Trump administration, Congress, and broader U.S. policy community should not take lightly.

UNINTENTIONAL BENIGN NEGLECT

For the past 15 years the United States has unintentionally adopted a policy of benign neglect toward the MDBs and the IMF. This is the result of a confluence of issues. Since the terror attacks of September 11, the U.S. foreign and national security apparatus has understandably focused its attention elsewhere. During the Bush administration this manifested itself at times in a somewhat thinly veiled mistrust of multilateral institutions that led the administration to question its value, fearing it acted contrary to U.S. interests and could constrain U.S. action. Early in his term in office this ideology was reflected in the internal debate over whether to support an IMF bailout for the pro-American government of President Fernando de la Rua of Argentina. Members of the administration, notably Treasury Secretary Paul O'Neill supported by a number of conservative intellectuals, believed that a large bailout would not help create a sustainable economy in Argentina and would reward the government for bad policies. This decision was not consequence free: it set in motion a series of events that led to the collapse of de la Rua's government and the eventual election of the Nestor Kirchner (and his wife, Christina) who took a decidedly anti-American track. This had real consequences for the Bush administration: Argentina under the Kirchner government would go on to scuttle the proposed Free Trade Agreement of the Americas.

This benign neglect is not limited to the Bush years. In 2010, the IMF, recognizing the need to adopt the institution to be more reflective of the changing distribution of global economic power, agreed to a series of reforms at the G-20 meeting in Seoul. These reforms focused on rebalancing the voting power of the IMF shareholders and became known as "IMF Quota Reform." These reforms primarily sought to shift voting power toward emerging and developing economies such as China, India, Brazil, and others, as well as give the IMF additional resources by shifting funds between internal accounts. With the changes in voting shares, the United States would retain its veto power over board decisions. The reductions largely affected European nations that remained overvalued relative to their economic size and contributions. The Obama administration hoped for quick congressional approval, but ran into opposition over a number of issues.

From the beginning, the Obama administration mishandled its relationship with the relevant congressional oversight committees. Second, in the past when administrations had gone to the Hill with complex asks around the multilateral institutions, it frequently required a significant investment of time on behalf of the Treasury secretary (and his or her senior staff) explaining to small groups of members of Congress why the asks were important and to seek their help. This did not happen initially with IMF Quota Reform. The result was a failure to secure quick passage in the U.S. Congress, and the reforms languished with little action taken for more than 5 years. The other 19 G-20 countries quickly passed the reforms within 1 year. Rather than aggressively push the reforms with Congress, the Obama administration allowed them to sit idle, until the security crisis in Ukraine required greater IMF involvement. As with the Bush administration's experience with the proposed IMF bailout of Argentina, the Obama administration's failure to act quickly with IMF Quota Reform had real-world consequences. At the same time, China used the four-year delay as political cover to create its own competing institutions such as the AIIB.

INCREASED COMPETITION

As middle-income countries, most notably China, earned a greater share of the global economy, new institutions emerged that provided increased competition for the MDBs. Fifteen years ago, for example, the World Bank, African Development Bank, and bilateral donors provided the vast majority of financing in sub-Saharan Africa. Other sources of financing—foreign direct investment, support from emerging economies, domestic resources, and commercial sources of debt—remained minuscule in comparison. But now countries have more domestic resources (growing from $100 billion in 2000 to just under $500 billion in 2014), access to international capital markets, and foreign direct investment (growing from $5.4 billion in 2000 to $54 billion in 2014). This has been replicated across developing and emerging market regions, and it means that the MDBs are no longer the sole source of development finance; they are now just one among many, making it difficult for recipient nations to discern their comparative advantage.

Former recipients of aid—China, India, and Brazil—are now making a mark by providing large amounts of financing to developing countries for infrastructure projects, something most of these countries desperately need. Against this backdrop, China sought to leverage its growing economic power (and disappointment over the failure of reform efforts) to create new multilateral institutions, launching the New Development Bank (colloquially known as the "BRICS Bank") and the AIIB. The former is largely an outlet for the BRICS (Brazil, Russia, India, China, South Africa) themselves, and it remains to be seen how much of an impact the NDB will have. The AIIB, in contrast, has attracted 57 countries and is seen as a viable entity (it has cofinanced four projects in its first year with the ADB, EBRD, and World Bank). It has an initial paid-in capital of $100 billion, making it roughly half the size of the World Bank and two-thirds the size of the ADB. The AIIB will not strictly adhere to the high environmental, social, and governance standards of the MDBs. This has the potential to create a competing system of less-stringent rules that would lower standards over time.

NEW PRIORITIES

Some have argued that for the MDBs to remain relevant in light of this new competition and an evolving global economic system, they must fundamentally change their focus. One recent report argues that the MDBs should become financiers for global public goods (e.g., climate finance, response to pandemics, and refugees). This is not necessarily wrong, but it also ignores many of the other priorities that may be more pressing for the MDBs on which to focus. It may also ignore the specific demands of its clients—developing countries. The World Bank is currently in the midst of a capital increase (seeking new pledged-in capital) as well as its triennial hat-passing exercise for its low-income soft loan entity, the International Development Association (IDA). This represents a moment for shareholders—led by the United States—to push for changes. From a thematic perspective, the MDBs need to consider the following:

Infrastructure Financing

Financing for infrastructure projects remains an important need across developing and emerging market countries. The MDBs already provide significant financing for infrastructure, but they need to redouble their efforts by ensuring that they meet their clients' demands in a timely manner. This will require examining how quickly they can approve requests for financing. MDBs should also continue to provide technical assistance for project preparation and strategic planning to ensure that the pipeline of bankable infrastructure projects is strong.

Private-Sector Development

The private sector is responsible for 9 out of 10 jobs created in developing countries; job creation and private-sector-led economic growth will help to end extreme poverty. The MDBs all provide a certain amount of private-sector financing through dedicated entities (e.g., the International Finance Corporation), but these need to look at where they are providing financing (i.e., a need to focus more on FCS) to ensure that they are targeting those most in need of their support.

Fragile and Conflict-Afflicted States

The majority of the world's poor live in fragile or conflict-afflicted states—countries that are least prepared to provide for their citizens and that attract low volumes or private investment. The World Bank and the regional development banks must begin to shift their resources toward these countries; this is especially critical to achieve the core purpose of the Sustainable Development Goals (SDGs): ending extreme poverty by 2030.

Importantly, though, this is not just about refocusing on new issues. The MDBs must also consider their internal operations and administration. Some of the tumult around the MDBs is a result of dissatisfaction with how they have approached their lending practices, neglected areas of focus, and general dissatisfaction with the speed of these organizations to process loans.

RENEWING U.S. LEADERSHIP

In the face of this competition, the MDBs have not been completely idle. The ADB, in response to the AIIB, made adjustments to its funding streams, creating an increase in the overall amount of money the ADB can lend. This is a good step and other MDBs should consider it as well. In spite of the lack of American focus on the MDBs over the past 15 years, the United States remains the largest or second-largest shareholder in all of the MDBs. It must exercise leadership in reforming what have become overly bureaucratic institutions and help to set them on the path of tackling the challenges of the next 15 years. The new administration should be prepared in its first year to offer a comprehensive road map on how it would overhaul the MDBs. This reform should center on a two-pronged approach:

1. New priorities: Continue to grow the infrastructure portfolio at all MDBs and ensure that the proper amount of technical assistance is available to support project preparation. Where appropriate, redirect MDB resources toward fragile and conflict-afflicted states and raise the profile of this issue by creating a vice president for conflict at the World Bank and the regional development banks. This will require that the MDBs also ensure that they are meeting their client demands in a timely manner.

2. Administrative systems: After 70 years, the MDBs have evolved into complex bureaucracies that each have their own unique internal cultures. Part of this includes the creation of world-class standards for environmental, social, and governance (human rights) protections. These should be maintained, but the MDBs need to consider how the rigid application of these principles frequently delays (often by many years) the implementation of critical projects. Any

review of the MDBs must include a top-to-bottom review of all lending practices and the bureaucratic mechanisms to ensure that these institutions continue to meet their customers' demands.

This will require presidential leadership and political capital. But the rewards justify it: the MDBs are at their heart American (and Western) institutions that have helped to spread the best of free markets and good governance. The United States should not lose sight of the fact that it has gained more from this system than it has lost. To solve the most difficult challenges of the next 15 years, the United States and its allies will need the help of the MDBs. This is an effort worth undertaking.

14. WILL THE TRUMP ADMINISTRATION SUSTAIN U.S. LEADERSHIP ON GLOBAL HEALTH?

J. Stephen Morrison

There are solid reasons to be hopeful that a Trump administration and Republican-controlled Congress will see the wisdom of continuing to sustain U.S. leadership in global health and that they may willingly choose to do so in concert with Democratic leaders in Congress and global health champions. That is true, notwithstanding the present uncertainty over what shape the Trump administration will take, who will fill key posts, and what the new administration's priorities will be.

On account of presidential leadership across several administrations, U.S. commitments to global health mushroomed to over $13 billion in the past decade and a half, accounting for one-third of U.S. foreign aid and a little more than one-third of total foreign assistance worldwide dedicated to health.

These investments have translated into verifiable, concrete, historic gains: the delivery today of antiretroviral therapy to over 8 million persons living with HIV; the reduction of malaria by one-third; the near-elimination of polio; and expanded access to maternal and child health and voluntary family planning services that have contributed to healthy timing and spacing of pregnancies, improved maternal health, and healthier infants.

Child survival in low-income countries has soared, as immunizations have become more widely accessible on a mass scale. On health security and pandemic preparedness, the United States was the single-most-indispensable force in rolling back the Ebola crisis in West Africa, protecting our own people at home, and assisting in building basic preparedness capacity in those low-resource countries that have no defenses against sudden outbreaks.

This is a legacy in global health whose logic reaches as far back as the Reagan era, when exceptionally strong commitments were made to foreign aid as a tool to do good in the world, among the poorest and most vulnerable, and were recognized as critically important in advancing U.S. national interests.

It is a legacy of success that reaches across Democrat and Republican administrations.

It is a legacy built on an unusual oasis of sustained bipartisan cooperation in Congress even at a time of hyper partisanship, backed by a broad coalition comprised of industry, the faith community, private foundations, implementing nongovernmental organizations, advocacy groups, and universities.

It is a legacy built on durable and proven structures of quality execution, accountability, and integrity: most notably, the President's Emergency Plan for AIDS Relief (PEPFAR) and the President's Malaria Initiative (PMI). The same is true for key international partner institutions: the Global Fund to Fight AIDS, Tuberculosis and Malaria (the Global Fund) and Gavi, the Vaccine Alliance.

It is a legacy erected on a powerful, pragmatic consensus that guides operations and choices:

- Foreign partner countries have to do more on their side; they need to own the agenda, ensure their leadership is committed at the highest levels, and budget a fair share of their own resources.
- Global health investments need to aim strategically to build enduring capacity in these countries and deliver measurable and sustainable results. Congress and the White House have to be convinced that U.S. dollars are translating into major health gains, and that U.S. national interests are served through the greater stability, prosperity, and growth of low-income countries, and through the improved

standing the United States achieves in the eyes of these countries' citizens.

- The private sector has to be at the center of forging solutions: devising new technologies and innovative approaches, joining public-private partnerships, and investing in the delivery of health services and the provision of medicines and medical products.
- U.S. investments have to be designed to motivate other donors to do their share. For example, every dollar the United States invests in the Global Fund—by law—is required to be matched by two dollars from other donors.
- There is a new consciousness, post-Ebola and Zika, that health security bridges the risks we see at home with those abroad. By definition, preparedness for new and reemerging dangerous infectious disease threats has to be holistic and long term. That includes battling the rise of antimicrobial resistance, a global problem that accounts for over 26,000 preventable deaths in U.S. hospitals each year.

These achievements require high-level political will, commitment over time, and real money: through PEPFAR, the United States has invested over $70 billion since it was launched in 2003.

The picture is certainly not always pretty or merely a celebration of victories. There are still 20 million persons living with HIV who do not have access to life-saving medications, and for whom there is no clear path to meet that need. The messaging over HIV/AIDS has often been excessively optimistic, which leads to confusion that can weaken resolve. Counting the number of people still on antiretroviral therapy has proven problematic, since so many fall off treatment, and needs to be tightened up considerably. Other donors, particularly in Europe, have lately reduced their commitments, owing to austere budgets and the immense cost of caring for expanded numbers of refugees: much more active U.S. diplomacy is needed to shore up their global health commitments. But these tough challenges do not diminish the enormous gains in health in low-income countries, spurred by strategic, sustained U.S. leadership.

That's the hopeful story, the business case for why the Trump administration needs to stay in the game. The other side of the story is more sobering: there are solid reasons to be worried that the incoming Trump administration and new Congress may turn away from the opportunity to sustain U.S. leadership in global health.

At home, there is no question we are heading into a period of intensified, bitter contestation over domestic health issues—centered on the Affordable Care Act, women's reproductive rights, the Supreme Court, and funding of groups such as Planned Parenthood. That carries the grave risk that these escalating confrontations could spill over into deliberations over the future of international programs, including family planning and reproductive health, where the United States has led for several decades and where any support of abortion is prohibited by law.

Intensified budget pressures could make the sustainment of U.S. leadership in global health highly problematic. A massive domestic stimulus bill, combined with a significant tax cut, could result in rising deficits, inflation—and acute pressures (stoked by populist sentiment) to cut foreign aid.

An "America First" approach could also be dangerous for U.S. global health equities. A Trump administration that decides to "go it alone" in any number of areas, and in the process alienates our partners and allies, could be highly disruptive of the many far-flung global health partnerships that the United States has forged over the past decade and a half with governments, civil society, the private sector, and the faith communities. That will be particularly true if the administration pursues a fiercely anti-Muslim posture in its immigration and counterterror policies, disinvests from UN agencies and multilateral institutions, defies international law prohibiting torture, and walks away from international alliances.

There are promising options, though. The Trump administration has within its reach several compelling opportunities that are strategic, that can leverage others to do more, that allow a large space for private-sector contributions, and that can advance U.S. national interests—and do good.

The president-elect's daughter Ivanka Trump has shown a particular interest in women's health issues. Adolescent girls and young women in low-income countries are a burgeoning population, with special needs in health and development. Getting them on to a pathway to improved health and education, including safe motherhood and better economic options as adults, will provide the underpinnings for stability, economic growth, healthy families, and stronger societies. The United States is well positioned, through its existing foundation of investments plus additional targeted programs, to keep them in schools; improve their health as mothers and that of their newborns; and secure their future as empowered, productive members of society. We have the tools to help them avoid unintended pregnancy and early marriage, space their pregnancies, prevent cervical cancer in the prime of their lives, and significantly improve their nutrition and that of their children.

We can leverage the deep and extensive U.S. investments in HIV/AIDS to significantly improve the prevention of HIV infection among adolescent girls and young women living in acutely dangerous "hot spots" where infection rates remain at staggeringly high levels.

We have the opportunity in the next four years to consolidate the elimination of polio across most of the globe, transition those programs to broader support of childhood immunization, and narrow the threat of polio in the few violent dangerous places where it is still found: Nigeria, Pakistan, and Afghanistan.

We have the opportunity to create a newly coherent U.S. approach to health security that can make Americans and the rest of the world safer from those dangerous outbreaks that are certain to occur. That will require budgeting ahead for these crises; strengthening White House oversight; and placing a new priority on battling antimicrobial resistance and new forms of resistance in TB, malaria, and HIV.

The time is ripe to turn high-level White House attention to tuberculosis. It has become the highest infectious disease killer globally, and dangerous forms of resistance are spreading rapidly. Yet for the first time in decades, the private sector is bringing forward promising new therapies and other technologies. And several countries with very high burdens—South Africa, Russia, India—are showing high-level interest in focusing anew the world's attention upon this destructive, neglected disease.

As the Trump administration and new Congress come into power, there are high stakes for the future of U.S. leadership on global health. Special attention and care are warranted. Neglect, missteps, and errant assaults on these historic achievements could have grave consequences both for the lives of millions whose health and development prospects have improved in partnership with U.S.-led efforts and for U.S. national interests.

The U.S. institutions that drive progress forward—the U.S. Agency for International Development, the Office of the Global AIDS Coordinator (overseeing PEPFAR), the President's Malaria Initiative—each require highly skilled, committed leadership of the quality that previous administrations, Republican and Democrat, provided, along with stable and predictable funding. The same is true for key international partners such as the Global Fund and Gavi, the Vaccine Alliance.

Even more important, the stage is set for the next administration and Congress to expand its leadership in global health in several areas, outlined above, where powerful, concrete gains can be achieved and verified in the course of the next few years. With high-level political will and sustained commitment, the Trump administration could create important new legacies in global health.

15. WHAT ROLE SHOULD VALUES PLAY IN AMERICAN STRATEGY?

James A. Lewis

> The dogmas of the quiet past are inadequate to the stormy present.
>
> *—Abraham Lincoln, Annual Message to Congress, December 1862*

American foreign policy is predicated on the familiar themes of a liberal international order sustained by American power and unquestionable in its intrinsic righteousness and ultimate success. But even before the election, a strong contrarian view of foreign policy had emerged in Washington after 15 years of failures in the Middle East, Asia, and Europe. We can summarize the conclusions behind this view as follows:

- The 25-year period of stability among major powers that followed the Cold War (and stability means that there is little incentive for any nation to use force or coercion to change its relations with other states) has ended.
- The era of unchallenged American dominance has also ended. Our challengers believe they are in a "strategic competition" with the United States and use unconventional or indirect tactics to circumvent U.S. power and hamper its ability to counter their actions.
- Unchallenged dominance afforded the United States the luxury to pursue foreign policies that made only marginal

contributions to advancing its vital interests. Dominance also led the United States to emphasize administrative and programmatic skills over strategic thinking, creating policies that were too often formulaic and feckless.

• The views of the foreign policy establishment no longer reflect the views or interests of many citizens.

This contrarian view is far from universal, and it confronts a stolid orthodoxy that, although shaken by the election, is still comfortable in its belief that recent events are only a temporary anomaly for the America Century. But an overwhelming case can be made that the foreign policies pursued since 2000 have damaged the United States, and in consequence, have also reversed the trend toward increasing democracy. We are in retreat. Reversing this decline and overcoming new challengers requires a clear assessment of American objectives, how they can be achieved, and at what cost.

Irrespective of the election, however, change in foreign policy will be forced upon us, a choice between renewed leadership or increased irrelevance. Let us be clear that change and recovery are possible. America may no longer be the unchallenged superpower, but it can be *primus inter pares* in the multipolar world many have long predicted. Numbers alone show this. The United States still has the greatest share of global income, a share that has only declined slowly in the last 60 years (from 28 percent in 1960 to 22 percent in 2015). It has the third-largest land mass. It is fourth in population size. Its research universities lead the world. America's military, although expensive, somewhat tattered after its misadventures, and overly reliant on its Cold War technological inheritance, retains conventional supremacy. The fundamentals of power put the United States in the top tier of nations, but being in the top tier does not guarantee influence nor the continued ability to set the agenda and direction of global affairs.

The problem is strategy, not resources or objectives. The long trajectory of American foreign policy has been shaped by the pursuit of a world ruled by law, democratic institutions, individual rights, and open markets. This American vision remains compelling. It serves both our own interests and the interests of other nations, reflecting ideals that America has acted on since it first became a world power, first in response to European imperialism, and then in the defense against totalitarianism. Critics will say that the pursuit of this vision has been erratic at best and too often sacrificed for self-interest, charges that have some truth to them, but no other nation has articulated an equally compelling vision of a just world order.

Our mistake was that we assumed this vision had prevailed with the Soviet collapse. Perhaps this could have been true if the United States had followed a less triumphalist and more astute foreign policy. Irrespective of this, we are now entering a period of renewed conflict, not over resources or territory or a conflict where military force will predominate, but a conflict over values and the international order they shape.

Powerful authoritarian nations strongly oppose this American vision. The collapse of the Soviet Union was the concluding event of a long ideological struggle that began in the 1930s. The situation we find ourselves in now is in good measure a reaction to victory in the Cold War and the American policies that followed it. Totalitarian ideologies were defeated, but Russia and China were not. Countries that were not democracies before the advent of communism did not magically become democracies upon communism's demise. The current generation of challengers is nimbler, bolder, and more dynamic in its pursuit of power at the expense of the United States. We have still not recovered from the damage to alliances and influence from the 2003 invasion of Iraq, and the decision to lead from behind was, in retrospect, simply a decision not to lead.

The motives that drive Russia and China are defensive and revanchist. Both wish to reclaim what they see as their rightful place in world affairs, but the fragility of their regimes and the fear the United States will exploit this is the ultimate source of their opposition. Their perception is that the United States, facing no constraints, will intervene to remake other nations in its own image with or without the approval of the United Nations. Their efforts to remake the U.S.-centric international order or to create alternatives to Western "information hegemony" are motivated by resistance to what they see as a comprehensive U.S. strategy for dominance. Iran and North Korea share these views, and these four nations will use unconventional means to damage U.S. influence. Their fears that they were the ultimate targets of regime change are now somewhat mitigated by their successes against the United States.

More importantly, our opponents reject "universal" values, the political and civil liberties contained in the Universal Declaration of Human Rights, calling them "Western." They would prefer to return to an earlier international order based on a nineteenth-century version of sovereignty, where a country is free to do as it pleases to its own citizens on its own territory. Their concerns over American disregard for sovereignty have some appeal to other nations who are uncomfortable with the unipolar moment. A world populated by powerful states untrammeled by international law and practice in their domestic actions is inherently unstable. The experience of the twentieth century showed that states that abuse their citizens do not make good neighbors.

Our opponents believe advances in U.S. military technology—the combination of unmanned vehicles, precision weapons, cyber-attack, and hypersonic strike—mean that in a conflict, the United States could achieve strategic effect against them, circumventing their defenses, even without using nuclear weapons. They have compensated for these advances by developing new strategies and tactics—covert, political, and unconventional—that can be used against the United States and its interests without triggering a damaging and perhaps unwinnable military confrontation.

We have entered a period of conflict, not necessarily military conflict and not a new Cold War—interconnected economies are a brake on sharp demarcations between hostile states. American military superiority means that conflict will involve political and "informational" aspects as much as the use of force. Although our opponents will prefer to avoid conventional military force to achieve their objectives, the risk of armed conflict is substantially increased, as our opponents are tempted by a perception of American weakness to seize the opportunity to coercively redefine the post–1945 world—in Syria, Crimea, the South China Sea, and perhaps elsewhere.

Some argue that universal values are utopian or that the United States cannot afford them when confronted by terrorism. Such thoughts reflect a misunderstanding of the nature of power. Force is at best a temporary substitute for ideas. In the contest between nation-states, power does not come from the barrel of a gun. Force has a role, but even the immensely powerful U.S. military cannot impose our values on other nations. The success of universal values, which seemed unassailable in 1989, has been reversed on the watch of the last two administrations, and rebuilding an effective foreign policy requires blending the pursuit of values with a willingness to use force and coercion in their service.

Reversing this decline will require that American policy adjust to the new era of strategic competition. Four questions can help us redefine American foreign policy:

- How do we accommodate regional powers without conceding democratic values?
- How do we defend the universal values now under attack?
- How do we change the 1945 international structure and its supporting institutions to reflect the end of transatlantic dominance and the emergence of new powers?
- What policies in trade and defense can be shown to the public to serve the interests of all Americans?

Answering these questions will require fundamental decisions on the direction of American foreign policy and a clear definition of truly vital interests, something that the United States has not had to do for two decades. Since so much of our opponents' strategy relies on the manipulation of information for both international and their domestic audiences, the United States must rebuild its capacity and credibility to counter the web of lies and mistruths designed to damage us.

As a starting point, America's vital interests can be described as promoting international stability and economic opportunity, and denying opportunities to use coercion and force against the United

States and its allies. These interests point to reasonable objectives: to pursue stability while rebuilding a modernized version of the framework and institutions for international order created by the United States and its allies.

Presidents and their administrations since Wilson have struggled to define policies that balance realpolitik and self-interest with idealism and justice. We have reached the end of a 25-year period of strategic stability and relative peace among major powers. The struggle of this new era may be again to assert and defend the universal values created after 1945. Our policies must adjust to this if they are to be effective.

INDEX

ABOUT THE EDITORS AND AUTHORS

Kimberly Breier is deputy director of the Americas Program and director of the U.S.-Mexico Futures Initiative at CSIS. She is a policy and intelligence professional with more than 18 years of experience on Western Hemisphere affairs, with particular expertise on Latin American politics. For the past five years, she has served as vice president of the boutique consulting firm Peschard Sverdrup International.

Mark Cancian is a senior adviser with the CSIS International Security Program. He joined CSIS in April 2015 from the Office of Management and Budget, where he spent more than seven years as chief of the Force Structure and Investment Division. Previously, he worked on force structure and acquisition issues in the Office of the Secretary of Defense and spent over three decades in the U.S. Marine Corps.

Victor Cha is a senior adviser and Korea Chair at CSIS and is a professor of government and director for Asian Studies at Georgetown University. From 2004 to 2007, he was director for Asian affairs at the White House, where he was responsible for coordinating U.S. policy for Japan, the two Koreas, Australia, New Zealand, and the Pacific Island nations. He also served as U.S. deputy head of delegation to the Six-Party Talks and as a senior consultant on East Asian security for different branches of the U.S. government.

Craig Cohen is executive vice president at CSIS. In this role, he serves as deputy to the president and CEO, responsible for overseeing and helping to achieve all aspects of the Center's strategic, programmatic, operational, outreach, fundraising, and financial goals, including recruitment of new program directors to CSIS. Previously, he served as vice president for research and programs, deputy chief of staff, and fellow in the International Security Program.

Heather A. Conley is senior vice president for Europe, Eurasia, and the Arctic and director of the Europe Program at CSIS. Prior to joining CSIS in 2009, she served as executive director of the Office of the Chairman of the Board at the American National Red Cross. From 2001 to 2005, she served as deputy assistant secretary of state in the Bureau for European and Eurasian Affairs with responsibilities for U.S. bilateral relations with the countries of northern and central Europe.

Anthony H. Cordesman holds the Arleigh A. Burke Chair in Strategy at CSIS. During his time at CSIS, Cordesman has been director of the Gulf Net Assessment Project and the Gulf in Transition Study, as well as principal investigator of the CSIS Homeland Defense Project. He has led studies on national missile defense, asymmetric warfare and weapons of mass destruction, and critical infrastructure protection. He also directed the CSIS Middle East Net Assessment Project and codirected the CSIS Strategic Energy Initiative.

Melissa G. Dalton is a senior fellow and chief of staff of the CSIS International Security Program (ISP). Her research focuses on U.S. defense policy in the Middle East, global U.S. defense strategy and policy, and security cooperation with U.S. allies and partners. As chief of staff, she advises the director of ISP on a broad range of strategic and management issues. Prior to CSIS, she served in the

Office of the Under Secretary of Defense for Policy from 2007 to 2014.

Josiane Gabel is vice president for programs and executive director of the Brzezinski Institute on Geostrategy at CSIS. Her previous positions at CSIS include executive officer to the president and CEO, director of executive education, and fellow in the Defense and National Security Group.

Matthew P. Goodman is senior adviser for Asian economics and holds the William E. Simon Chair in Political Economy at CSIS. Previously, he served as director for international economics on the National Security Council staff. Before joining the White House, he was senior adviser to the undersecretary for economic affairs at the U.S. Department of State.

Michael J. Green is senior vice president for Asia and Japan Chair at CSIS and chair in modern and contemporary Japanese politics and foreign policy at the Edmund A. Walsh School of Foreign Service at Georgetown University. He served on the staff of the National Security Council from 2001 through 2005, first as director for Asian affairs and then as special assistant to the president for national security affairs and senior director for Asia.

Shannon N. Green is director and senior fellow of the Human Rights Initiative at CSIS and managing director of CSIS's Commission on Countering Violent Extremism. Prior to joining CSIS, she was senior director for global engagement on the National Security Council staff. She also worked at the Center of Excellence on Democracy, Human Rights, and Governance at the U.S. Agency for International Development.

John J. Hamre is president, CEO, and Pritzker Chair at CSIS. Before joining CSIS, he served as the 26th U.S. deputy secretary of defense and undersecretary of defense (comptroller). In 2007, Secretary of Defense Robert Gates appointed him to serve as chairman of the Defense Policy Board.

Todd Harrison is director of the Aerospace Security Project and a senior fellow in the International Security Program at CSIS. He joined CSIS from the Center for Strategic and Budgetary Assessments, where he was a senior fellow for defense budget studies. He previously worked at Booz Allen Hamilton in the aerospace industry and served in the U.S. Air Force Reserves.

Andrew Hunter is a senior fellow in the International Security Program and director of the Defense-Industrial Initiatives Group at CSIS. Previously, he served as a senior executive in the Department of Defense, as well as chief of staff to the undersecretary of defense for acquisition, technology, and logistics. He also served as a professional staff member of the House Armed Services Committee.

Christopher K. Johnson is a senior adviser and holds the Freeman Chair in China Studies at CSIS. An accomplished Asian affairs specialist, he spent nearly two decades serving in the U.S. government's intelligence and foreign affairs communities and has extensive experience analyzing and working in Asia on a diverse set of country-specific and transnational issues.

Sarah O. Ladislaw is a senior fellow and director of the Energy and National Security Program at CSIS, where she concentrates on the geopolitics of energy, energy security, energy technology, and climate change. She previously worked in the Department of Energy's Office of Policy and International Affairs, where she covered a range of economic, political, and energy issues in the Western Hemisphere.

James A. Lewis is a senior vice president and director of the Strategic Technologies Program at CSIS. He is an internationally recognized expert on cybersecurity who has authored numerous publications on the relationship between technology, innovation, and national power. Previously, he was a member of the U.S. Foreign Service and Senior Executive Service.

Scott Miller is senior adviser and holds the William M. Scholl Chair in International Business at CSIS. From 1997 to 2012, he was director for global trade policy at Procter & Gamble, a leading consumer products company. In that position, he was responsible for the full range of international trade, investment, and business facilitation issues for the company.

J. Stephen Morrison is senior vice president and director of the Global Health Policy Center at CSIS. Earlier, he served in the Clinton administration, as committee staff in the House of Representatives, and has taught for 12 years at the Johns Hopkins University School of Advanced International Studies.

Olga Oliker is a senior adviser and director of the Russia and Eurasia Program at CSIS. Her recent research has focused on military, political, economic, and social development in countries in transition, particularly in Russia, Ukraine, and the Central Asian and Caucasian successor states to the Soviet Union. Prior to CSIS, she held a number of senior posts at the RAND Corporation.

Daniel F. Runde is director of the Project on Prosperity and Development and holds the William A. Schreyer Chair in Global Analysis at CSIS. His work centers on the central roles of the private sector and good governance in creating a more free and prosperous world. Previously, he led the Foundations Unit for the Department of Partnerships & Advisory Service Operations at the International Finance Corporation.

Conor M. Savoy is deputy director and fellow with the Project on U.S. Leadership in Development and the Project on Prosperity and Development at CSIS. He focuses on the day-to-day management of the two projects, as well as implementing and guiding their research agenda. His research includes the role of the private sector in international development, governance and rule of law, trade and investment, and development finance.

Amy Searight serves as senior adviser and director of the Southeast Asia Program at CSIS. From 2014 to 2016, she served as deputy assistant secretary of defense for South and Southeast Asia. Prior to that, she was principal director for East Asian security at the Defense Department and senior adviser for Asia at the U.S. Agency for International Development.

Andrew Shearer is senior adviser on Asia-Pacific security and director of the Project on Alliances and American Leadership at CSIS. Previously, he was national security adviser to Prime Ministers John Howard and Tony Abbott of Australia, where he played a leading role in formulating and implementing Australian foreign, defense, and counterterrorism policies.

ABOUT CSIS

For over 50 years, the Center for Strategic and International Studies (CSIS) has worked to develop solutions to the world's greatest policy challenges. Today, CSIS scholars are providing strategic insights and bipartisan policy solutions to help decisionmakers chart a course toward a better world.

CSIS is a nonprofit organization headquartered in Washington, D.C. The Center's 220 full-time staff and large network of affiliated scholars conduct research and analysis and develop policy initiatives that look into the future and anticipate change.

Founded at the height of the Cold War by David M. Abshire and Admiral Arleigh Burke, CSIS was dedicated to finding ways to sustain American prominence and prosperity as a force for good in the world. Since 1962, CSIS has become one of the world's preeminent international institutions focused on defense and security; regional stability; and transnational challenges ranging from energy and climate to global health and economic integration.

Thomas J. Pritzker was named chairman of the CSIS Board of Trustees in November 2015. Former U.S. deputy secretary of defense John J. Hamre has served as the Center's president and chief executive officer since 2000.

CSIS does not take specific policy positions; accordingly, all views expressed herein should be understood to be solely those of the authors.

www.ingramcontent.com/pod-product-compliance
Lightning Source LLC
Chambersburg PA
CBHW050536270326
41926CB00015B/3256